Cinderella

A Pantomime

Paul Reakes

A SAMUEL FRENCH ACTING EDITION

FOUNDED 1830

SAMUELFRENCH.COM
SAMUELFRENCH-LONDON.CO.UK

© 2008 by Paul Reakes

CINDERELLA is fully protected under the copyright laws of the United States of America, the British Commonwealth, including Canada, and all other countries of the Copyright Union. All rights, including professional and amateur stage productions, recitation, lecturing, public reading, motion picture, radio broadcasting, television and the rights of translation into foreign languages are strictly reserved.

ISBN 978-0-573-16428-6

www.samuelfrench.com
www.samuelfrench-London.co.uk

FOR PRODUCTION ENQUIRIES

UNITED STATES AND CANADA
Info@Samuelfrench.com
1-866-598-8449

UNITED KINGDOM AND EUROPE
Theatre@Samuelfrench-London.co.uk
020-7255-4302

Each title is subject to availability from Samuel French, depending upon country of performance. Please be aware that CINDERELLA may not be licensed by Samuel French in your territory. Professional and amateur producers should contact the nearest Samuel French office or licensing partner to verify availability.

CAUTION: Professional and amateur producers are hereby warned that CINDERELLA is subject to a licensing fee. Publication of this play does not imply availability for performance. Both amateurs and professionals considering a production are strongly advised to apply to the appropriate agent before starting rehearsals, advertising, or booking a theatre. A licensing fee must be paid whether the title is presented for charity or gain and whether or not admission is charged.

For professional/stock licensing enquiries, please contact Samuel French.

No one shall make any changes in this title for the purpose of production. No part of this book may be reproduced, stored in a retrieval system, or transmitted in any form, by any means, now known or yet to be invented, including mechanical, electronic, photocopying, recording, videotaping, or otherwise, without the prior written permission of the publisher. No one shall upload this title, or part of this title, to any social media websites.

MUSIC USE NOTE

Licensees are solely responsible for obtaining formal written permission from copyright owners to use copyrighted music in the performance of this play and are strongly cautioned to do so. If no such permission is obtained by the licensee, then the licensee must use only original music that the licensee owns and controls. Licensees are solely responsible and liable for all music clearances and shall indemnify the copyright owners of the play(s) and their licensing agent, Samuel French, against any costs, expenses, losses and liabilities arising from the use of music by licensees. Please contact the appropriate music licensing authority in your territory for the rights to any incidental music.

IMPORTANT BILLING AND CREDIT REQUIREMENTS

If you have obtained performance rights to this title, please refer to your licensing agreement for important billing and credit requirements.

CHARACTERS

Cinderella
Baron Beaujolais, Cinderella's father
Baroness Beaujolais, Cinderella's stepmother
Mattie, Cinderella's stepsister
Hattie, Cinderella's stepsister
Buttons, the family servant
The Duke Of Verruca
Nip, the Duke's henchman
Tuck, the Duke's henchman
Archie, the Duke's nephew
Prince Charming
Old Beggar Woman (really **the Fairy Godmother**)
Urk, the jailer
Kathy
Messenger
Major-Domo
Chorus of **Townsfolk**, **Children**, **Cat** and **Kittens**, **Fairies**, **Coachman** and **Horses**, **Servants** and **Guests** at the ball

SYNOPSIS OF SCENES

ACT I
SCENE 1 Outside the Baron's house
SCENE 2 A street
SCENE 3 A glade in the Royal Forest
SCENE 4 The street
SCENE 5 The Stepsisters' dressing-room
SCENE 6 The Baron's kitchen

ACT II
SCENE 1 The palace ballroom
SCENE 2 A dungeon cell
SCENE 3 In the ballroom
SCENE 4 The street
SCENE 5 Hall of the Baron's house
SCENE 6 The bit before the last bit
SCENE 7 The Grand Finale

Time — 18th century

MUSICAL NUMBERS

ACT I

No 1	Song and Dance	Townsfolk
No 2	Comedy Duet	Mattie and Hattie
No 3	Song and Dance	Buttons, Cinders and Townsfolk
No 3a	Reprise of No 1	Townsfolk
No 4	Song and Dance	Cinders and Townsfolk
No 5	Solo	Prince
No 6	Song and Dance	Cinders and Townsfolk
No 7	Solo	Cinders
No 7a	Reprise of No 2 (Optional)	Mattie and Hattie
No 8	Cat Dance	Cat and Kittens
No 9	Duet	Prince Charming and Cinders

ACT II

No 10	Song and Dance	Guests
No 11	Comedy Song	Archie and Guests
No 12	Comedy Dance	Mattie, Hattie and Archie
No 13	Song and Dance	Prince Charming, Cinders and Guests
No 13a	Reprise of No 13	Prince Charming, Cinders and Guests
No 14	Comedy Song and Dance	Mattie, Hattie, Buttons and Kathy
No 14a	Reprise of No 7	Cinders
No 15	Song and Dance	All
No 16	House Song	Buttons, Duo

COPYRIGHT MUSIC

The notice printed below on behalf of the Performing Right Society should be carefully read if any other copyright music is used in this play.

The permission of the owner of the performing rights in copyright music must be obtained before any public performance may be given, whether in conjunction with a play or sketch or otherwise, and this permission is just as necessary for amateur performances as for professional. The majority of copyright musical works (other than oratorios, musical plays and similar dramatico-musical works) are controlled in the British Commonwealth by the PERFORMING RIGHT SOCIETY Ltd, 29-33 Berners Street, London W1P 4AA.

The Society's practice is to issue licences authorizing the use of its repertoire to the proprietors of premises at which music is publicly performed, or, alternatively, to the organizers of musical entertainments, but the Society does not require payment of fees by performers as such. Producers or promoters of plays, sketches, etc., at which music is to be performed, during or after the play or sketch, should ascertain whether the premises at which their performances are to be given are covered by a licence issued by the Society, and if they are not, should make application to the Society for particulars as to the fee payable.

A separate and additional licence from PHONOGRAPHIC PERFORMANCES LTD, 1 Upper James Street, London W1R 3HG, is needed whenever commercial recordings are used.

CHARACTERS AND COSTUMES

Cinderella, (Principal Girl) known to her friends as Cinders, is a petite and beautiful young woman. Despite the cruel treatment she suffers at the hands of her stepmother and stepsisters, she still manages to radiate kindness, grace and charm without feeling sorry for herself. She should not be portrayed as soppy or simpering. She is hard done by, but has learned to live with it. A good singing voice and dancing ability is called for. Her everyday costume is picturesquely ragged and patched. A spectacular ballgown, with jewellery, slippers, etc. is required for the transformation scene before she goes to the ball. Magnificent Finale costume.

Baron Beaujolais is Cinderella's father. This poor man is completely under the thumb of his second wife, the Baroness. Any attempt at standing up for himself, or Cinderella, has been long since abandoned. However, he is not above making the occasional derogatory remark when he thinks he can get away with it. No singing is required, but he does have to perform a comic dance with the Major-Domo in the ballroom scene. He also gets a bit tipsy at the ball. His attire, no doubt chosen for him by the Baroness, is elegant, but worn untidily. He also gets to wear a long nightshirt and tasselled nightcap.

Baroness Beaujolais is the ultimate in formidable battleaxes. She treats Cinderella like dirt, dominates her husband, and generally bosses everyone about. She dotes on her two obnoxious daughters, but even gives them orders when necessary. She is also a colossal snob, looking down her nose at the audience, and fawning over the Duke and the "Prince". No singing or dancing is required. All her costumes are flamboyantly extravagant. Her ballgown has an extra long train. She also gets to wear a nightgown, robe and frilly nightcap.

Mattie and **Hattie** (played by males) are the ugly stepsisters. Extreme sibling rivalry is very much in evidence, particularly when it comes to attracting men. They constantly bicker, squabble and deride each other's appearance. However, they are strongly united when it comes to insulting anyone else, including the audience. Fortunately, they are such a ridiculous pair that we are saved from disliking them too much. Ideally, Mattie should be large and "well-upholstered", while Hattie should be tall and skinny. Comedic singing and dancing ability is required. It goes without saying that all their costumes, make-up and hairdos, etc. are outrageous and funny. Their outfits for the ball being the *piéce de résistance*. Although the story is set in the eighteenth century, their costumes can reflect the more outlandish trends and fashions of the present day. Monumentally ridiculous Finale costumes.

Buttons is the family servant. He and Cinderella are great friends — and nothing more. He despises the way she is treated and tries to stand up for her, losing his job in consequence. He should be a likeable and charismatic character. Singing and dancing ability is an advantage, but good rapport and camaraderie with the audience is essential, particularly with the youngsters. His costume is the traditional uniform with buttoned tunic and pill box hat. Special Finale uniform.

The Duke of Verruca is the megalomaniac dictator who has seized power in the absence of the rightful heir to the throne. On hearing of Prince Charming's imminent return, he devises a cunning plan which will allow him to continue ruling the country in his own particularly nasty way. This devious and thoroughly unpleasant individual never misses an opportunity of goading the audience into a frenzy of boos and hisses. No singing or dancing ability is required, but a strong and dominant personality is needed. His costume, although elegant, should be of unrelieved black, giving him a sinister and forbidding appearance. He wears a sash with stars and orders for the ballroom scene.

Nip and Tuck (The Duo) are the Duke's hapless henchmen. These are a likeable pair of nitwits who live in fear of their nasty boss. Determined not to be part of his evil plans any longer they are continuously trying to do a "runner". From the start they should be on very friendly and confidential terms with the audience. Singing and dancing ability is an advantage, but good participation with the audience is essential. They wear a uniform of sorts which looks comical and ill-fitting. For the ballroom scene they add distinctive looking cloaks and hats with tall plumes.

Archie is the Duke's nephew. This young man defiantly falls into the "nice but dim" category. To use an old-fashioned theatrical term, this is a "silly ass" part. Archie and Bertie Wooster share a lot in common, except that Archie is penniless and is forced to impersonate a royal prince by his scheming uncle. He should endear himself to the audience from the start, and gain their sympathy. Singing and dancing ability is an advantage, but good character portrayal and the use of an affected "utter class" accent is essential. His costume should convey a look of shabby gentility. For the ball scene he is arrayed in a very princely outfit with embroidered coat, silk breeches and powered wig, etc.

Prince Charming (Principal Boy) is a young man who certainly lives up to his name. Handsome, debonair, courteous and good-humoured, he is charm itself. Even after losing his memory, and having to work for the Baroness, he still manages to retain all his excellent qualities. A charismatic personality with a good singing and dancing ability is required. His costume, for a prince, is rather plain and is shabby and travel-stained. He gets to wear a natty version of the Buttons uniform with buttoned tunic and pill box hat. Both of these costumes do little to conceal his gorgeous pair of legs! Magnificent Finale costume.

Old Beggar Woman. She is really the magical Fairy Godmother in disguise. As the beggar, she appears old and stooped, her voice weak and trembling. When she is revealed as the Fairy Godmother, she is upright, graceful and speaks with a strong yet pleasant voice. She must radiate magic. No singing or dancing required. Her beggar costume consists of a long, all enveloping hooded cloak which is ragged and patched. This conceals her magnificent fairy costume which is revealed after a flash and black-out. She will also require a shining wand.

Kathy is the pretty young woman who brings Buttons his food in the dungeon cell. It is her idea to use "ghosts" as a way of scaring off the jailer and enabling Buttons to escape. She even dons a white sheet and pretends to be one! Later they disguise themselves as the Duo in order to help the Prince. Although there isn't time for romantic dalliances it should be obvious that she and Buttons have fallen for each other in a big way. After all, he does announce they are going to be married! Singing and dancing ability is an advantage. Her costume is plain homespun, but very neat and tidy. She wears an apron which is removed after they leave the cell. Pretty Finale costume.

Urk, the Jailer, is a huge, hairy, lumbering lout. He is slow-witted and converses mainly in grunts. For all his brutishness, he is very scared of ghosts. His is also very scared of the ugly sisters, but then, who can blame him? No singing or dancing required. His costume should be rough and grimy. It consists of thick baggy tights, a leather jerkin and a wide belt to hold a bunch of large keys and a vicious looking club.

The Messenger, who brings the letter telling of Prince Charming's return, can be played by a male, female or child. Dressed as Footman if male, Maid if female, Pageboy if child.

The Major-Domo, attired in fine livery, needs to have a loud, clear voice. He should be very dignified and haughty. This will make his dance with the Baron look even sillier.

The **Chorus**, **Dancers** and **Children** have plenty to do appearing as Townsfolk, their Children, Cat and Kittens, Fairies, Coachman and Horses, Servants and Guests at the ball.

PRODUCTION NOTES

STAGING

The pantomime offers opportunities for elaborate staging, but can be produced quite simply if funds and facilities are limited.

There are five full sets:
    Outside the Baron's house
    A glade in the Royal Forest
    The Baron's kitchen
    The Palace ballroom
    Hall of the Baron's house

There is one half-set:
The Stepsisters' dressing-room

These scenes are interlinked with two frontcloth scenes:
    A street
    A dungeon cell

There can be a special Finale setting or the palace ballroom scene can be used.

The Transformation Scene Act I, Scene 6

As this is such a well known part of the Cinderella story, the audience will be anticipating something truly magical to happen. Please don't disappoint them and try to make it as spectacular as facilities and funds will allow. It is the only scene in the pantomime that requires the use of flashes, special sound and lighting effects, and a quick "before your very eyes" scenic change. The following is only a suggestion of how the transformation can be achieved in a simple way. Individual directors who know the capabilities of their own stage will certainly have their own ideas. The coach and horses are pre-set behind the kitchen backcloth. During the black-out, the prop pumpkin is removed, the Cat and Kittens exit, and the backcloth is flown. Needless to say, all this must be achieved as quickly and as quietly as possible. Behind the coach is the town backcloth or a lit cyclorama. The pumpkin-shaped coach will depend on the space available. It can be a flat cut-out, outlined with small lights, or a more elaborate three dimensional affair. The horses (we won't talk about using real ones!) can also be cut-outs or models, but would be best represented by two children or members of the Chorus in stylized white horse costumes.

Hall Of The Baron's House Act II, Scene 5
This setting requires a large walk-in cupboard on one side, and a large open fireplace on the other. Both are used as hiding places during the frantic chase scene that ensues, so they need to be firm and stable. The fireplace should be high enough to allow characters to dash in and out without having to bend down too much. The cupboard has a door and looks fairly shallow. It should be fixed to the side wing with an opening in the back giving access to offstage. At one point it appears that seven characters are all hiding in the cupboard at the same time! It is advisable to have these pieces well in use before the actual performance.

The Sisters' Slapstick Scene Act I, Scene 5
A slapstick routine for Mattie and Hattie opens the scene. Each sister tries to sabotage the other's attempts at making herself look beautiful for the ball. There is a lot of messy fun involving make-up, face creams, powder and hair sprays, etc. A protective floor covering is advisable! During the business, they remove their dressing gowns to reveal ludicrous underwear. There are more comical capers as they try to lace up each other's corsets. The actual business and ad-lib for the routine is left to the director and his two performers. However, it should be carefully thought out and well rehearsed. There is nothing worse than slap dash slapstick!

Paul Reakes

Other works by Paul Reakes
published by Samuel French Ltd

Pantomimes

Babes in the Wood
Bluebeard
Dick Turpin
Goody Two Shoes
King Arthur
King Humpty Dumpty
Little Jack Horner
Little Miss Muffet
Little Red Riding Hood
Little Tommy Tucker
Old Mother Hubbard
Robinson Crusoe and the Pirates
Santa in Space
Sinbad the Sailor

Plays

Bang, You're Dead!
Mantrap

ACT I
Scene 1

Outside the Baron's house

Prominently at R *is the front of the Baron's house with a practical door. There are other housefronts* L. *The backcloth and groundrow show the rest of the town with a distant view of the Royal Palace. There are entrances* R *and* L

When the CURTAIN *rises, the Townsfolk are discovered. They go straight into the opening song and dance*

Song 1

Mattie (*off; yelling*) Out the way! Mind yer backs! I'm comin' through! Weeeee!

The Townsfolk move quickly aside as Mattie, mounted on a scooter, shoots on from L

She does a lap of the stage, narrowly missing the toes of the Chorus. It ends with her crash-landing R, *and falling over. The Townsfolk laugh*

Ahhhgh!! (*She sits up; painfully*) Cor! I bet that buckled me big end! (*To the Chorus*) What are you lot laughin' at? (*She gets to her feet; calling*) Hattie? Where are ya? (*Bellowing*) HATTIE!

Hattie, also mounted on a scooter, enters L. *She is trying to be more ladylike and sedate about it. With one leg raised in the air, she does a lap of the stage, then comes to a wobbly halt beside Mattie*

What happened to you? You're all behind.
Hattie Ooh! Hark who's talking! (*Pointing to Mattie's prominent posterior*) Miss Chubby Cheeks 1775!
Mattie Are you incinerating that I'm fat?
Hattie No, but if you fell over you'd rock yourself to sleep trying to get up again!
Mattie At least I've *got* a figure! I don't look like a walking ironing board! What took you so long getting here?

Hattie Oh, I got held up in (*she says the name of a local street*). They're diggin' up the road again! And of course — (*preening herself*) all the workmen started calling out and doing wolf whistles.
Mattie Yes. I think they've lost their dog!
Hattie And when they saw *you* they thought they'd found it!

They glare at each other for a moment, and then Mattie turns to a small boy

Mattie Oy! You, Bruce Willis!
Boy (*coming down to them*) Me?
Mattie Yes, you! (*Handing him the two scooters*) Put these in our backyard!
Boy (*making for the exit* DR) Right!
Mattie And no riding on 'em!
Boy Course not. I haven't got an HGV licence!

The Boy exits DR *and the Townsfolk exit in various directions*

Mattie That was facetious, wasn't it?
Hattie How should I know what his name is!
Mattie Children these days, eh! It was very different when I was little.
Hattie Little? You were never little, sister dear. They had to get all your school uniforms from rent-a-tent! (*She laughs*)
Mattie And they got yours from MFI! In *flat packs*!

As Mattie turns away and laughs, Hattie catches sight of the audience. She gapes at them, open-mouthed, and then sidles up to Mattie

Hattie There's something you should know, Mattie.
Mattie What's that, Hattie?
Hattie We're being scrutinized.
Mattie Really? I never felt a thing.
Hattie (*pointing to the audience*) Look!

Mattie and Hattie come forward and peer out at the audience

Mattie Oooh! It's a lot of people! I *think* they're people!
Hattie What a funny looking bunch!
Mattie There's all sorts out there! There's women. There's little girls. There's little boys. There's ——
Hattie Men! (*Getting excited*) MEN! MEN!

Act I, Scene 1

Mattie (*pushing Hattie*) Oh, stop it, will ya! (*To the audience*) You'll have to forgive my sister. She's man-mad! I can't think why. They never give her a second look!

Hattie Oh, yes, they do! (*She does a sexy walk up and down the stage*)

Mattie You're right. They can't believe their eyes the first time!

Hattie (*continuing the walk*) I'm always turning men's heads.

Mattie To say nothing of their stomachs! (*Referring to Hattie's walk*) Oh, stop doing that! Give the flies a chance to settle! Anyhow, you've got it all wrong, Sis. It's *me* the men look at! They're always giving me the once over.

Hattie Yes! Once and it's all over!

Mattie Me with my — (*running her hands down her sides*) lovely hour glass figure! (*She strikes a sexy pose*)

Hattie Mmn. What a shame all the sand's gone to the bottom! (*She laughs*)

Mattie Anyway, Sis, we're far more beautiful and better dressed than that lot out there! Trinny and Susannah would have a field day with them!

Hattie You're right, Sis! Ugh! Just look at 'em! (*Pointing someone out in the audience*) Especially *that* one!

Mattie Ooh, yes! You can see she doesn't go to (*local hair/beauty salon*)!

Hattie No. You'd have to go to Kwik-Fit to achieve a look like that!

Mattie (*pointing to someone else in the audience*) And what about *her*?

Hattie Oh dear, oh dear! What *has* she got on?

Mattie Someone should tell her that Halloween's over.

Hattie And I bet they spent hours getting all dressed up to come here.

Mattie I know. What a complete waste of time.

Hattie (*to the audience*) Just face it, losers, you'll never be as gorgeous as us.

Mattie Not in a million years. We're the tops!

Hattie We're the best! And to prove it ...

They signal to the Pianist/Conductor

Song 2

Mattie There! That proves we're the best, doesn't it?
Audience No!
Hattie Oh, yes, we are!
Audience Oh, no, you're not.
Hattie Oh, yes, we are!

Audience Oh, no, you're not.
Mattie Oh, they're as common as muck! And green with envy.
Hattie And when we get into that new gear we bought, they'll be even greener.
Mattie That reminds me! Where are those two with our shopping? (*Bellowing*) Cindrella!
Hattie (*squawking*) Buttons!
Mattie (*bellowing*) CINDERELLA!
Hattie (*squawking*) BUTTONS!

Still bellowing and squawking, they exit L

Buttons and Cinderella enter DR, *both carry bulging clothes shopping bags*

Cinders Was that Mattie and Hattie calling for us, Buttons?
Buttons Either that or someone was squeezing a baby elephant.
Cinders I expect they're looking for their shopping. Oh, dear. That means I'll be in the doghouse again.
Buttons Don't worry, Cinders. I'll deal with those two. I'll tell them we had to hire a forklift truck to carry all their stuff.

They put the bags down

Cinders They like buying a lot of things, don't they?
Buttons Yes, except the things they really need.
Cinders What's that?
Buttons Paper bags to put over their heads! Those two ought to be arrested for passive ugliness.
Cinders (*smiling*) You really shouldn't say things like that, Buttons.
Buttons I was being polite. And the way they dress! Crikey! Talk about mutton dressed as lamb. They're revolting! And the way they treat you ...
Cinders Oh, please, don't start that again.
Buttons Well, it's true. They treat you worse than they treat me, and I'm only a servant. You're their stepsister, and they treat you like a doormat. And as for that old boot, the Baroness!
Cinders Buttons, you shouldn't talk about my stepmother like that.
Buttons Why not? She's worse than they are. And she never gives you a penny. When was the last time you had a new dress? You've been wearing that one since *Coronation Street* was just a footpath. (*Getting heated*) They're a load of rotten, nasty —
Cinders Shh! (*Indicating the audience*) We've got company.

Act I, Scene 1   5

Buttons Eh? (*Looking at the audience*) Oh, so we have! Where did they come from? Hello, folks! (*To Cinders*) I think they've dozed off. (*To the audience*) I said — Hello, folks!
Audience Hello.
Buttons That's more like it. Are you all right? Great. Well, this is Cinders. Short for Cinderella.
Cinders (*to the audience; waving*) Hello, everyone.
Buttons And I'm Buttons. Short for ... Buttons. Please forgive my outburst just then. But it really makes my blood boil the way they treat poor Cinders. Have you seen her ugly stepsisters?
Audience Yes.
Buttons You couldn't very well miss them, could you? They're horrible, aren't they? I call them the gruesome twosome!

Mattie and Hattie enter L

Mattie Ah! There they are!
Buttons (*seeing them and grimacing*) Ugh! (*To the audience*) Who needs to watch *Primeval*? (*This can be substituted with another TV show*)
Mattie Who gave you permission to talk to this riff-raff?
Buttons Don't call them that. They're very nice, and —
Hattie How dare you answer back, you measly minion, you!
Mattie Yes! You forward flunky, you!
Hattie Where's our shopping?

Buttons and Cinders pick up the bags. The Sisters snatch them away and look in them. Buttons and Cinders take this opportunity to sneak towards an exit

Mattie Oi! You two! Not so fast! Where's my Oil of Ugly?
Hattie And where's my Nivia's Village?
Cinders Aren't they in the bags?
Mattie }
Hattie } (*together*) No!
Cinders Oh, dear. I must have left them in the shop.
Mattie }
Hattie } (*together; an outraged squeal*) Left them in the shop!
Cinders I'm very sorry.

Threateningly, the Sisters close in on poor Cinders

Mattie You're a stupid girl! What are you?

Cinders A stupid girl.
Hattie You're a useless twit! What are you?
Cinders A useless twit.
Mattie You're a ——
Buttons (*stepping in*) Hey! Leave her alone! (*To Mattie*) Why don't *you* go and hire yourself out as a dartboard?
Mattie Ooh!
Buttons (*to Hattie*) And why don't *you* go and take a long walk off a short pier?
Hattie Ooh!
Buttons And when you've done that, you can both go and boil your heads!
Mattie
Hattie } (*together*) Ooh!
Mattie You just wait 'til we tell our mummy what you said!
Buttons Go ahead and tell her! Do I look bovvered?
Mattie (*bellowing*) Mummy!
Hattie (*squawking*) Mummy!

They continue bellowing and squawking as the Baroness comes out of the house. She is followed by the Baron

The Townsfolk enter from various directions, curious to know what all the noise is about

Baroness Silence! (*Bellowing*) SILENCE!

There is dead silence

Baron (*yelling*) Silence!

The Baroness glares at the Baron

Sorry, dear.
Baroness Girls, what is the meaning of this uncalled-for cacophony?
Mattie Oh, Mummy! That nasty servant was being rude to us!
Hattie Yes, Mummy. He told us to go and boil our heads!
Baron (*chuckling*) That's a good one!

The Baroness glares at the Baron

Sorry, dear.
Baroness (*to Buttons*) Is this true? Have you been disrespectful to my daughters?

Act I, Scene 1

Buttons (*proudly*) Yes!
Baron Good show!

The Baroness glares at the Baron

Sorry, dear.
Baroness I cannot allow this insolence from servants. You will apologize to them at once.
Buttons (*defiantly*) No, I won't!
Baroness (*outraged*) What?
Buttons They were being horrible to Cinderella. (*Indicating the audience*) Ask them. (*To the audience*) They were bullying poor Cinders, weren't they, kids?
Audience Yes.
Buttons They were being really mean to her, weren't they?
Audience Yes.
Baroness Enough! (*She surveys the audience and sneers at them*) Huh! I fail to see that *their* opinion matters. Who are these peasants anyway?
Mattie They were nasty to us as well, Mummy!
Hattie Yes, Mummy, they were!
Baron (*to the audience; giving them a thumbs-up*) Good show!
Baroness (*snappily*) Be quiet!
Baron Yes, dear.
Baroness Unfortunately, I have no authority over them. I wish I had. They seem a very unruly rabble. (*To Buttons*) But I do have authority over *you*. You will apologize to my daughters at once, or cease to remain in my employment.
Cinders (*to Buttons*) You'd better do as she says or you'll lose your job.
Buttons I'll never apologize to that pair of botoxed bimbos!
Mattie }
Hattie } (*together*) Sack him, Mummy! Sack him!
Buttons (*advancing on the Baroness*) And while I'm on the subject, I've got a few things to say to *you!* Cinders is your stepdaughter and you treat her like dirt. You're nothing but a stuck up toffee-nosed old trout!
Baroness Ooh! How dare you! I've never been so insulted in all my life!
Buttons Go on. With a face like that you must have been.
Baroness Cedric, are you just going to stand there and let him talk to me like this?
Baron (*smugly*) You told me to be quiet, dear.

Baroness (*to Buttons*) Your services are no longer required! Go! You are dismissed!
Mattie *Sacked*!
Hattie *Fired*!
Buttons That suits me.
Cinders Oh, Buttons. (*Pleading to the Baroness*) Please give him another chance.
Baroness I will not! (*To Buttons*) I never want to see your face again.
Buttons And I certainly don't want to see yours. (*To the Sisters*) Or yours!
Baroness I will see to it that you never get employment in this town again. Come, girls!

The Baroness marches to the house door

> *Mattie and Hattie follow, jeering at Buttons, and poking their tongues out at him. They also do the same to the audience, then exit into the house*

The Baron goes to Buttons

Baron (*holding out his hand*) I'm sorry about this, old chap.
Buttons (*shaking his hand*) It's not your fault, Baron. You can't help it if you remarried during a total eclipse.
Baroness Cedric!
Baron Yes, dear.

> *The Baron scuttles across the stage and the Baroness pushes him into the house. She exits, slamming the door after her*

Cinders Oh, Buttons. You've lost your job because of me. I'm so sorry.
Buttons You've got nothing to be sorry for, Cinders. That pesky pair had it coming to them.
Cinders But what will you do now?
Buttons I'll find something. Even if I have to go to (*local place*). I don't care what happens to me, it's you I'm worried about. Left at the mercy of Cruella and the toxic twins. What will you do?
Cinders I suppose I'll just have to put up with it.
Buttons You don't have to. Why don't you come away with me?
Cinders I can't leave Father.
Buttons I hate to say this, Cinders, but your dad's already a condemned man. You can see the thumb print on his head for miles.
Cinders I know. That's why I still have to stay with him.

Act I, Scene 1

Buttons Who knows, perhaps I'll make my fortune and I'll come back and take you away from all this.
Cinders Oh, I'll miss you, Buttons.
Buttons And I'll miss you, Cinders.

Song 3

After the number, Buttons bids a sad farewell to Cinders and exits DL

Cinders is waving to Buttons

Old Beggar Woman enters from DR. *She goes amongst the Townsfolk, begging. They all shun her and exit in various directions*

The Old Beggar Woman moves down to Cinders

Old Woman Good-day, my dear.
Cinders (*turning to her*) Oh! Hello. Can I help you?
Old Woman Can you spare a few pennies for a poor old woman to buy some food?
Cinders I'm afraid I haven't got any money. If I had, I'd willingly give it to you. I'm very sorry.
Old Woman (*turning away*) That's all right, my dear.
Cinders (*stopping her*) Please wait. I might not have any money, but I can find you some food.
Old Woman You're very kind, Cinderella.
Cinders How do you know my name?
Old Woman I ... I must have heard them calling you.
Cinders I'll take you to the kitchen. You can warm yourself by the fire while I prepare you something to eat.
Old Woman You're kindness itself, Cinderella.
Cinders Don't mention it. (*Taking the Old Beggar Woman's arm*) This way.

She leads the Old Beggar Woman out DR

Music plays

Nip and Tuck (The Duo) enter US. *They do a comic march around the stage. They bump into each other, etc. Eventually, Nip moves* DR, *and Tuck* DL

The music stops, and they stand to attention. A fanfare sounds

The Duke of Verruca enters US, *and comes* DS. *His sinister appearance should provoke boos and hisses from the audience*

Duke Ah! What it is to be popular! (*He sneers at the audience*) Why, what have we here? Nip and Tuck!
Nip }
Tuck } Sir!
Duke What is this curious collection of cretins I see before me?
Nip (*giving the audience a quick look, then shrugging*) Dunno!
Duke (*to Tuck*) Do you know?
Tuck (*doing the same as Nip*) Nope!
Duke (*snarling at them*) Well, make it your business to find out, you dozey dunderheads!
Nip Right. (*To the audience; waving*) Hello!
Audience Hello!
Tuck (*to the audience; waving*) Hello!
Audience Hello!
Nip Are you all right?
Audience Yes!
Tuck What do you think of it so far?
Audience Rubbish!
Nip They've got good taste, haven't they?
Duke Enough of this! I did not ask you to make friends with them! I asked you to find out who they are!
Nip Right. (*To the audience*) Do you know who you are?
Audience Yes!
Nip (*to Duke*) Yes. They know who they are.
Tuck They're very bright, aren't they? They must go to (*local school/college*)
Duke You fools! Tell them who I am! Tell them *what* I am!
Nip Oh, I think they already know what *you* are!
Duke What was that?
Nip (*cowering*) Nothin'.
Duke Bah! If (*current baddie*) had to put up with you two, he'd get a job on *Songs of Praise*! Tell these pathetic pustules who I am!
Nip Right. (*To the audience*) He is the Duke of Verruca.
Tuck (*aside*) A right pain in the foot!
Nip He's a —
Duke Don't bother! I will tell them myself. (*To the audience*) When the king died a year ago I took over ruling this kingdom. All the wealth and power is now mine! People do as I say! And if they don't, I make them suffer! (*To the Duo*) Don't I?
Nip }
Tuck } (*together; grimacing; to the audience*) Oh, yes, he does!

Act I, Scene 1   11

Duke So be warned! Do not fall foul of me! My power is absolute! My word is law! And I love every minute of it! (*He gives his evil laugh*) Ha! Ha! Ha! That's better. I like to have a good laugh first thing in the morning. It means I can spend the rest of the day being thoroughly unpleasant!

The Baroness comes out of the house. She is followed by the Baron

The Townsfolk enter from various directions and fill the back and sides of the stage

The Baroness sees the Duke, and rushes to him

Baroness (*fawning*) Oh, Duke! Your Grace! (*She curtsies*) What a lovely surprise.
Duke Not for me, it isn't. Who are you, madam?
Baroness I am Baroness Beaujolais. Surely you remember me. We met last month at the (*local*) WI cake-making competition. You sampled my flapjacks.
Duke Ah, yes. And I remember the stomach ache which followed.
Baroness Er, yes. This is my husband, Baron Beaujolais. Cedric! Greet His Grace.
Baron (*aside; to the Baroness*) Do I have to? He gives me the creeps.
Baroness (*glaring at the Baron*) Do it!
Baron Yes, dear. (*He bows to the Duke*)
Baroness To what do we owe this great honour, Your Grace?
Duke I have never visited this particular quarter of the town before. I like to be familiar with all the districts in my kingdom.
Baron Your kingdom? Don't you mean, Prince Charming's kingdom?

There are murmurs of agreement from the crowd which does not go unnoticed by the Duke

Duke (*advancing on the Baron*) Explain yourself!
Baron Well ... He is the rightful ruler ... He's the heir to the throne, isn't he?
Townsfolk (*advancing a little*) Yes. That's true. He's right. (*They ad-lib*)

The Duke turns on the Townsfolk, and they retreat

Duke What you say is perfectly true, Baron, but answer me this. Do you see Prince Charming here? (*To the crowd*) Do any of you see him here? (*Snarling*) Well, do you?

The Townsfolk sadly shake their heads. The Duke sneers

No, I thought not. As a small boy the Prince was sent abroad to school. When his education was complete, he decided to travel and see the world. He has not been seen or heard of for years. His father has been dead for over a year now, and has he been in contact with us? No. Has he returned to claim the throne? No. It is obvious he cares nothing for the kingdom or his responsibilities. In his absence someone has to rule the country. And that someone is *me*! Have you any objections? (*To the Baron; snarling*) Well?

Baron No, dear! Er ... I mean ——

Duke (*to everyone*) And while I'm on the subject of ruling — I am thinking of increasing the taxes.

There are groans and protests from the crowd

(*With evil relish*) I thought you'd be pleased. And on that happy note, I will now take my leave. (*He turns to go*)

Baron Good job, too.

Duke (*turning back*) What was that?

Baron I said ... (*With a pathetic wave*) Toodle-oo!

Baroness (*still sucking up to him*) Your Grace, before you go, I would like you to meet my daughters.

Baron (*aside*) That'll wipe the smile off his face.

Baroness I'll just give them a little call. (*Bellowing towards the house*) MATTIE! HATTIE!

They all react to this

Baron (*to the Duke*) That's nothing. You should hear her when she shouts.

Mattie and Hattie come out of the house. They have changed into more outrageous costumes

Baroness Ah, here they are. (*Bringing Mattie and Hattie over to the Duke*) Looking as lovely as ever. Your Grace, allow me to present my daughters. This is Mattie, my eldest.

Mattie You've got that wrong, Mummy! (*Indicating Hattie*) *She's* the eldest. (*To the Duke*) You've only got to look at her. She's got crow's feet big enough to plant potatoes in!

Hattie And you've only got to look at *her!* She's got a spare tyre that'd get you to Australia and back!

The Sisters glare at each other, nose to nose

Act I, Scene 1

Baroness (*pulling the Sisters apart*) Girls! Girls! (*To the Duke; making light of it*) They're so competitive. (*She pulls the Sisters aside*) Stop showing yourselves up. Don't you realize who that man is?
Mattie Dracula's grandad? (*Or topical gag*)
Baroness He's the Duke of Verruca! He now rules the country.
Mattie Does that mean he's loaded?
Baroness Yes. So you must be very nice to him.
Hattie How nice?
Mattie Is he single?
Baroness Yes.
Hattie (*preening herself*) Then he's all mine!

Hattie does her sexy walk, moving towards the Duke

Mattie (*pulling Hattie out of the way*) Ger off!

They get on either side of the Duke, and move in close. He finds this unpleasant, to say the least

Hattie (*fluttering her eyelashes; in her sexy voice*) Hello, Dukey.
Mattie (*doing the same*) Hello, you ravishing ruler, you.
Hattie I don't believe I've had the pleasure.
Duke (*grimacing*) And you're not likely to.
Mattie I expect you find it very hard.
Duke I beg your pardon?
Mattie Ruling a whole country by yourself.
Duke I manage.
Hattie You know what you need, don't you?
Duke At the moment — air rescue!
Hattie No. You need to look for a good woman.
Mattie And you need look no further. This way! (*She pulls his face in her direction*)
Hattie (*pulling his face in her direction*) This way!

This is repeated a few times until the Duke, with an angry roar, pulls himself free

Duke Enough of this! Do you seriously imagine that I would consider either of *you* for a wife?
Mattie } (*together; affronted*) Oooo! Get him!
Hattie }
Duke *I*, who have the pick of any woman in the kingdom! Even (*current "looker"*) would be mine for the asking!
Mattie She's not that desperate. (*Or topical gag to suit*)

Hattie Well, it's your loss, mate!
Mattie Yeah! You don't know what you're missing,
Duke Oh, I think I do. If I want to give myself nightmares I can watch *Supernatural*!

A Messenger, carrying a letter, rushes on from DL

Messenger (*going straight to the Duke*) Your Grace! Your Grace! This letter has just arrived at the Palace.

The Duke takes it and reads. With an angry growl, he screws the letter up

Mattie Must be his bill from the off-licence.
Hattie Or a refusal from (*current "looker" mentioned earlier*) Ha! Ha! That'll teach him!

Angrily, the Duke pushes Mattie and Hattie aside, and exits at the back

The Duo scuttle out after him

Baroness What do you suppose was in that letter to make him so angry?
Messenger I know! I had a read of it first. It's really good news. For us, at least. It's from Prince Charming!

There is a reaction from everyone

He's returning home. And he'll be arriving this very afternoon!

This greatly pleases everyone and they all chatter, excitedly

Cinders and the Old Beggar Woman enter DR

Cinders What's happened?
Baron Great news, Cinders. We've just heard that Prince Charming is coming home this afternoon. (*Jubilantly*) Happy days are here again!

The Baroness notices the Old Beggar Woman

Baroness Cinderella!
Baron I spoke too soon!

Act I, Scene 1   15

Baroness Who is that disreputable looking person? I hope you have not been feeding the poor again.
Old Woman (*aside; to Cinders*) I'll deal with this, my dear. (*Moving to the Baroness*) It's all right, lady. I asked her for some food, but she refused to give me any.
Baroness I should hope so indeed. Go away at once!

The Old Beggar Woman moves away to L

Come, girls! Let us prepare ourselves for the Prince's return. We must go and put on our faces. (*She moves to the house*)
Baron (*aside*) Someone else's would be better!
Baroness (*turning*) What was that?
Baron I said — good news in that letter!

The Baroness pushes the Baron into the house and they exit

Mattie I wonder what Prince Charming looks like?
Hattie Oh, he's bound to be a great big gorgeous hunk.
Mattie Yes! A bit of Brad Pitt and with a dash of David Beckham!
Hattie And a dollop of David Dimbleby!
Mattie David Dimbleby?
Hattie Well, we'll have to talk at some point.
Mattie That needn't bother you, Sis! *You* won't be in the running. Once the Prince sets eyes on me, he won't be able to see anyone else.
Hattie That's very true. You ought to carry a "wide load" notice!

Mattie chases Hattie into the house

Cinders goes to the Old Beggar Woman

Cinders Thank you for not telling my stepmother that I gave you something to eat.
Old Woman It's not for you to thank *me,* my dear. You saved me from starving.
Cinders If you come back tomorrow I'll find you some more food.
Old Woman Bless you, Cinderella, bless you.
Baroness (*off; bellowing from the house*) CINDERELLA!

Cinders runs into the house

The Old Beggar Woman watches her go, then turns to address the audience

Old Woman That poor girl. She is kindness itself, and yet they treat her so cruelly. It's very unfair, isn't it?
Audience Yes.
Old Woman Well, fear not, it is within my power to bring about a change. Cinderella will soon find happiness in her life. How? Ah, that will be revealed later on.

The Old Beggar Woman exits L

The Townsfolk come forward to sing and dance

Reprise of Song 1

At the end of the number, the Lights fade to Black-out

Music covers the scene change

Scene 2

The Lights come up on a street

There are tabs, or a frontcloth showing picturesque houses and shops. There are entrances DR *and* DL

Buttons enters DR

Buttons (*to the audience*) Hello, folks! Hi, kids! I'm just on my way to find a new job. I'm really worried about poor Cinders though. Are those two ugly sisters still being nasty to her?
Audience Yes.
Buttons It's rotten, isn't it? I wish there was something I could do to help her. Still, there is some good news. I hear that Prince Charming is coming home. Is that right?
Audience Yes.
Buttons Well, I'd better be on my way. (*He moves* DL) Wish me good luck.
Audience Good luck.
Buttons Oh, come on. I shall need more good luck than that.
Audience (*much louder*) Good luck!
Buttons That's more like it. Thanks, folks. Bye!

Waving to the audience, Buttons exits DL

The Duo enter DR

Act I, Scene 2   17

Nip Hey, look! (*Indicating the audience*) They're still here.
Tuck Course they are. (*TV Show*) isn't on tonight. (*To the audience*) You haven't seen our boss, have you?
Nip You know who we mean. Old face ache! The Duke of Puke!
Tuck We're trying to keep out of his way at the moment.
Nip Yes. He's in a fouler mood than usual.
Tuck All because Prince Charming is coming back.
Nip That means he won't be able to rule the country any more.
Tuck Or boss people about.
Nip It's great news.
Tuck It is. Better than when (*topical gag*)!
Nip As you may gather, we both hate the Duke.
Tuck And we hate working for him.
Nip We only took this job because we couldn't get in at (*local firm*).
Tuck So, until the Prince takes over, we're keeping out of Mr Nasty's way.

Archie enters DL. *He looks about him, obviously lost*

Tuck Hey! Who's that?
Nip I dunno. I've never seen him before.
Tuck He looks lost. Why don't we try communicating with him?
Nip Better not. Let's try talking to him first.

They move to Archie

Nip
Tuck } (*together*) Hello.
Archie (*turning*) Oh! Hello! I say! I wonder if you can help me. I'm in the most awful quandary.
Nip Your hat's pretty terrible, as well.
Tuck What seems to be the trouble?
Archie I'm looking for someone. My uncle, actually.
Nip Uncle Actually? That's a funny name.
Archie No, actually isn't his name.
Nip Oh, I see! (*He finds this highly amusing, and gives a prolonged laugh*)
Archie (*to Tuck*) I say! Is he all right?

Nip's laughter subsides

Tuck What's his name?
Archie How should I know, old chap. He's your friend.

Tuck No, what's your uncle's name?
Archie Sebastian!
Nip There's no need to be like that!
Archie That's his name. Uncle Sebastian.
Tuck I've never heard of anyone around here called Sebastian.
Nip Nor me.
Archie You probably know him by his title. He's the Duke of Verruca.
Nip
Tuck } (*together; reacting*) The Duke of Verruca!
Archie Does that ring a bell?
Nip Yes! A dirty big clanger.
Archie Do you know him?
Tuck Oh, we know him all right! We work for him.
Nip He's our boss. Come to think of it, that name suits him. He's a right Sebastian!
Archie What awfully good luck. Will you take me to see him?
Tuck Are you sure you want to?
Archie What do you mean?
Tuck When did you last see your uncle?
Archie Oh, not for years and years. Not since I was just a tiny tot. I can't say I was very keen on him. He was frightfully bossy and stole my sweeties, as I recall. But I don't suppose he's like that anymore.
Nip
Tuck } (*together*) Not much!
Archie The fact is, I'm rather down on my luck at the moment. I haven't got a bean. I was hoping Uncle Sebastian might help me out.
Tuck Oh, he'll do that all right!
Nip Yes! Right through the nearest window!
Archie So, will you take me to him?
Tuck Yes, but be warned. He's not a very affable man.
Nip No, he's a very horrible man!
Archie Oh, I'll chance that. I'm sure he'll be absolutely delighted to see his long lost nephew.

The Duo exchange looks

Tuck This way.

The Duo lead Archie to DR

What's your name, by the way?
Archie It's Archie, actually.
Nip Archie Actually? That's a funny name ... Oh, I see!

Act I, Scene 2   19

He does the prolonged laugh again. They wait for it to subside

Tuck He can't help it. His father spent a lot of time in (*local place*)!

They exit DR

The Duke enters DL. *He is met with a barrage of boos and hisses*

Duke (*to the audience; snarling*) Grr! Still here making the place look untidy, are you? Bah! Silence! I said — (*yelling*) silence! (*To someone in the audience*) That includes *you*! So! Prince Charming is returning to claim the throne, is he? Curse him! That means my days of wealth and power are over! No longer will I be able to bend people to my will! No longer will I be able to afford to live at (*local expensive area*)! Bah! It's not fair, is it?
Audience Yes!
Duke Oh, no, it isn't!
Audience Oh, yes, it is!
Duke Oh, no, it isn't!
Audience Oh, yes, it is!
Duke Well, until it happens I am still in command! And if I have any more trouble from you, I will dump you all in my deepest dungeon! Oh, yes, I will!
Audience Oh, no, you won't.
Duke Oh, yes, I will.

The Duo and Archie enter DL

Tuck Your Grace?
Duke (*breaking off from his dispute with the audience*) What is it, you fool? Can't you see I'm getting the better of these puny little parasites! (*To the audience; snarling*) Grrr! Grrr!!
Nip (*to Archie*) That's your uncle. The Mary Poppins of (*local place*)!
Tuck (*to the Duke*) We've brought someone to see you.

They push Archie forward. The Duke looks at him with disgust

Duke Who is this bonneted buffoon?
Archie Nunkie! (*He rushes to the Duke and throws his arms around him*)
Duke (*pushing him away*) How dare you! How dare you manhandle a man of my mighty magnificence! Don't you know who I am?
Archie You're my Uncle Sebastian! My Nunkie! I'd recognize you anywhere. That nose! Those eyes! That ...

The Duke scowls at him

Lovely smile! Don't you remember me, Nunkie? I'm your nephew! I'm little Archie!
Duke Nephew? (*He peers at Archie*) Ah, yes ... yes ... I recognize you now. You were a very peculiar looking infant. And you don't seem to have improved with age!
Archie (*holding out his arms*) Nunkie!
Duke (*retreating*) Keep away from me! What are you doing here? What do you want?
Archie I've come to see you, Nunkie.
Duke Well, now you've seen me — go *away!*
Archie The thing is, Nunkie, I'm a bit down on my luck at the moment.
Duke (*snarling at him*) I see! You've come here hoping for a hand out, have you?
Archie That would be awfully sweet of you.
Duke In case you hadn't noticed, I'm not an awfully sweet person. You won't get a penny out of me!
Archie Oh, I see. Well, perhaps you could give me a job.
Duke A job! What can *you* do? You don't look capable of doing anything! Listen! I am *not* giving you any money. And I am *not* giving you a job.
Archie (*disappointed*) Oh.
Duke But I *am* going to give you a piece of good advice.
Archie (*brightening*) Oh, yummy!
Duke It's this. (*Snarling at him*) *Clear off!* I never want to see your face, or any other part of you, here again! Do you understand?
Archie (*crestfallen*) Yes, Nunkie.
Duke Then — *get out!* (*Giving his unpleasant laugh, he moves away*)
Nip
Tuck } (*together; sighing*) Ahhh!

The Duo move to Archie and encourage the audience to "Ahhh!" for him

Nip We told you he was a rotten old nasty.
Archie It's a bit thick. I can understand him not wanting to give me money and all that, but he needn't have been so frightfully off with me. I am his nephew, after all. I bet if I were a lord or a prince or something, he wouldn't have been so jolly rude.

The Duke reacts to this

Act I, Scene 3

Goodbye, you chaps. It's been a pleasure meeting *you* anyway. And your friends out there. Thoroughly nice types, all of them. (*Waving to the audience*) Bye!

Nip
Tuck } (*together*) Bye, Archie.

Archie moves to exit

Duke Wait! (*Moving across to Archie*) What did you say just then?
Archie (*turning*) Who, me? I said they were thoroughly nice types.
Duke Before that! Something about a prince?
Archie Oh, that! I said you wouldn't have been so rude to me if I was a prince or something.
Duke A prince! (*He looks Archie up and down, a plan forming in his devious brain*) Yes, yes ... It might work ... It *will* work! Tell me, did anyone else see you arrive here?
Archie Not a soul.
Duke Let's keep it that way. (*He puts his arm around Archie*) Nephew, I think I'm going to find a use for you, after all.
Archie (*pleased*) Oh, jolly good! Are you going to give me a job?
Duke I am! The best job in the country! The top job, in fact!
Archie (*delighted*) Oh, say! Thanks awfully! What is it?
Duke You'll soon find out! (*To the audience*) And so will you!

Doing his evil laugh, the Duke takes Archie out DL

With very puzzled expressions, the Duo look at each other, then at the audience. They shrug, and follow the others out

Lights fade to Black-out

Music covers the scene change

Scene 3

The Lights come up on a glade in the Royal Forest

Full set. The wings and ground row represent trees and bushes. The backcloth shows the forest with a distant view of the Royal Palace. There are tree stumps that can be used as seats

Cinders and the Townsfolk are discovered. They go straight into a colourful song and dance

Song 4

After the number, the Baroness and the Baron enter R

Baroness (*viewing the Townsfolk*) Ah! Splendid! I see you have all made an effort to look presentable for Prince Charming's return. All except you, Cinderella! You look a disgrace!
Cinders I'm sorry, Stepmother. But this is the only dress I have.
Baron Excuse me, dear.
Baroness Why? What have you done?
Baron Nothing, dear. If you gave Cinders some money she could buy herself a new dress. It's just a suggestion.
Baroness Don't be absurd! And do not be suggestive again.
Baron No, dear. Sorry, dear.
Baroness (*to Cinders*) You must keep in the background when the Prince arrives. It would be most unbecoming for one of my household to be seen looking like *that*. Now, where are Mattie and Hattie? I don't want them to miss the Prince's arrival. (*Bellowing*) MATTIE! HATTIE!

Everybody reacts

(*To the Baron*) Do you think they heard me?
Baron In New Zealand, dear.
Baroness What?
Baron I said loud and clear, dear.

Mattie and Hattie enter R. *They are now wearing even more outlandish outfits*

Baroness You look lovely, girls. I'm sure the Prince will be impressed.
Mattie Well, he will with *me*. Tatty Hattie here won't get a look in!
Hattie That's what you think, Fatty Mattie!
Baroness I'd like to think that one of you will catch the Prince's eye.
Mattie Why? Is he throwing it about?
Baroness I am talking about matrimony. One of you could be our future Queen.
Mattie / **Hattie** (*together; squealing with delight*) Oooooo!

The Duke enters R. *He is followed by the Duo*

Baroness Your Grace. (*She curtsies*)
Mattie / **Hattie** (*together*) Your Grease!

Act I, Scene 3   23

The Sisters try to curtsy, but make a complete mess of it

Baroness Has the Prince arrived yet, Your Grace?
Duke I have just received news that he is entering the forest. He will be here at any moment.

There is general excitement from the others

Silence! I have decided that it will be more appropriate if I meet the Prince alone.

There is dissension and disappointment from the others

Baroness May I ask why, Your Grace?
Duke You may not, madam. It is my decision and therefore cannot be questioned. You will all leave now. (*To the Duo*) Remove this rabble!

The Duo herd the protesting Townsfolk out on both sides

(*To the Baroness and Sisters*) That includes you!

The Baroness and Sisters exit R

The Duke glares at the Baron, who scuttles out after them

(*To the Duo*) Have they all gone?
Nip }
Tuck } (*together*) Yes, sir.

Archie pops up from behind a bush

Archie Can I come out now, Nunkie?
Duke No, you fool! Get out of sight!

Archie disappears behind the bush

The Duke moves to L *and looks off. The Duo are obviously feeling very unhappy about something. They get into a quick huddle, and then cross timidly to the Duke*

Tuck Er ... Duke?
Duke (*Still looking off* L) What is it?
Tuck Nip and I would like to ... hand in our notice.

Duke (*turning; with a snarl*) What?
Nip We don't agree with what you're planning to do.
Duke So!

The Duke advances on the Duo and they retreat

> Let me tell you how it is, you pair of backsliding buffoons! If you do not carry out my orders you will wish you had never been born! I know where you live! And I know where your mummies and daddies live! I even know where your grannies live! Do you understand? (*Snarling*) Well?

Nip
Tuck } (*together; terrified and murmuring*) Yes, sir.

Duke I can't hear you!

Nip
Tuck } (*together; louder*) Yes, sir.

Duke Good! (*He goes back* L, *and looks off*)
Nip (*to Tuck*) That went well, didn't it?
Duke Here comes the Prince! Curses! He's got someone with him! Never mind. We'll deal with him as well! (*Approaching the Duo*) Get out of sight. When I give the signal, you know what you have to do! Don't let me down or it'll be worse for you! Get out!

He pushes them off at the back

Archie pops up from behind a different bush

Archie Can I come out now, Nunkie?
Duke (*pushing Archie out of sight again*) No! (*To the audience; with an evil chuckle*) Ha! Ha! Soon my plan to retain power will be put into action! It won't be long now!

Chuckling, he sweeps out R

The handsome Prince Charming and Buttons enter L. *The Prince is rather shabby and travel-stained*

Buttons (*to the audience*) Hello, folks! Hi, kids! I'm back again. Your good luck wishes certainly worked. Look who I met on the way. Prince Charming himself! (*To the Prince*) These are some of my friends, Your Highness.
Prince And very pleased I am to meet them. (*To the audience*) Greetings!

Act I, Scene 3   25

Buttons We got chatting, and guess what? He's given me a job. I'm to be his personal ballet.
Prince (*smiling*) Valet.
Buttons Valet. It's a sort of manservant. I'm very grateful to you, Your Highness.
Prince Not at all. I can tell you're a splendid fellow and will make an excellent general factotum.
Buttons Thanks for that. Whatever it means. Well, are you glad to be back in your own country after all these years?
Prince Indeed I am. Since leaving here as a small boy, I have travelled the wide world. I have seen many wonderful and exotic places. But in my dreams I always returned here. It is sad that my return should be under such unhappy circumstances.
Buttons Your father?
Prince Yes. I only received the news of his tragic death a month ago. I returned as fast as I could. Hence my rather disreputable appearance.
Buttons I hope you won't find it dull here after your travels abroad.
Prince I have done with travelling, Buttons. It is now time to settle down and face up to my responsibilities.
Buttons Is there anyone you'll miss? A sweetheart perhaps?
Prince (*smiling*) Alas, no. There is no sweetheart, Buttons. In all my travels I have never found love.
Buttons Well, perhaps you'll find it here. You know the old saying — east or west, home is best.
Prince You could be right. It would be nice to find someone. Very nice indeed.

Song 5

Buttons It's a good thing you've come home, Your Highness. The country is in a terrible state since that tyrant took over.
Prince Tyrant? Tell me more.
Buttons Well, he's —

The Duke enters R

Just walked in!
Duke (*moving to the Prince; very smarmy and bowing low*) Your Highness! Welcome. Welcome home.
Prince And you are?
Duke I am the Duke of Verruca, Your Highness. Since the sad demise of your father it has been my great honour and privilege to look after the running of the county.

Buttons (*aside; to the Prince*) Looking after himself more like! Don't trust him.

Prince (*to the Duke; rather curtly*) Thank you for bridging the gap during my absence. But now the responsibility of ruling the kingdom will be mine. (*Pointedly*) And mine alone.

Duke (*fawning*) Of course, Your Highness, of course.

Prince I must confess I am a little disappointed that there are not more here to welcome my return.

Duke So am I, Your Highness. It's disgraceful. But you know how fickle these peasants are. There may be one or two loitering about. I will ascertain.

He bows and moves to the back. Unseen by the others, he signals off R

The Duo enter, carrying clubs

The Duke mimes hitting the Prince and Buttons. He pushes the Duo forward, and they creep up behind the unsuspecting pair

Prince (*during the above business*) I see what you mean, Buttons. I wouldn't trust that man an inch.

By now the audience will be shouting warnings

Audience Behind you!

Buttons (*to the audience*) What's wrong? Behind us? (*He looks behind them and sees the advancing Duo*) Your Highness! *Look out!*

The Prince turns. To suitable music, a struggle ensues between the Prince, Buttons and the Duo. The Duke remains in the background. The struggle is quite short lived as the half-hearted Duo is no match for the Prince and Buttons. They are pushed to the ground and drop their clubs

The music stops. As the Prince and Buttons haul the Duo to their feet, the Duke picks up one of the clubs, and creeps up behind the Prince

Buttons (*seeing this*) Look out!

The Duke hits the Prince on the head. He falls to the ground, unconscious

Buttons (*lunging at the Duke*) You!

Act I, Scene 3

Duke Seize him!

The Duo grab Buttons and hold him firmly

Buttons (*struggling in their grip*) You won't get away with this! Whatever it is!
Duke (*smirking*) Oh, I think I will. (*To the Duo*) Take him to the palace and lock him in the deepest dungeon. I will decide his fate later on. Now, get him away from here before the others return! *Go!*

The Duo drag the struggling Buttons out L

(*To the audience; with an evil chuckle*) Ha! Ha! The first part of my master plan is now complete! That other fool is a complication, but he will not be around long enough to interfere!

Archie pops up from behind yet another different bush

Archie Can I come out now, Nunkie?
Duke (*snarling at him*) No!

Archie ducks out of sight again

(*Looking down at the prone Prince*) Now to dispose of you, my fine friend!

The Duke is about to drag the Prince away, when voices are heard off R

Curses! Someone is coming! I can't be found here with him like this! Curse and double curse!

He dithers, and then runs out L

Mattie and Hattie enter R, *followed by Cinders*

The Sisters are too busy waffling to notice the Prince. Cinders does, and she crosses to kneel beside him

Mattie When the Prince gets a whiff of my new perfume he'll be blown away.
Hattie That stuff could blow away a herd of elephants! Phew!
Mattie It's better than the Harpic you use! (*She sees the Prince*) Hey! What's goin' on 'ere?

The Sisters move over and look down at the Prince

Hattie Ooo! It's a man! *A young* man!
Mattie What's he doing down there?
Cinders I'm not sure. I ... I think he's unconscious.
Hattie Unconscious? I told you that perfume was lethal!
Cinders Perhaps you'd better go and get some help while I stay with him.
Mattie She's right. He's no use to either of us in that state, is he?
Hattie No. We like our men wide awake and fully active!

Mattie and Hattie exit R

The Prince starts to regain consciousness. Cinders helps him to sit up

Cinders Hello.
Prince Who ... Who are you?
Cinders My name's Cinderella. What happened to you?
Prince (*dazed and confused*) I ... I don't know ... (*He feels his head and winces*) Oh! My head hurts!
Cinders What's your name?
Prince My name? My name? I ... I don't know ... I can't seem to remember ...
Cinders How did you get here?
Prince I don't know that either. All I can remember is opening my eyes and seeing you. (*Gazing at her*) And I can't think of a better reason for opening them.
Cinders (*embarrassed*) Er ... Do you think you can stand up?
Prince If you'll help me ... er ... Cinderella. Did you say that was your name?
Cinders Yes. (*She helps him get to his feet*)

The Duke enters L. *He pulls up short at seeing the Prince and Cinders together*

The Duke is about to creep away, when Cinders sees him

(*Calling out*) Please! Can you help? I found this young man lying on the ground. He was unconscious. I think he must have hit his head. He can't seem to remember who he is or how he got here.
Prince It's quite true, I'm afraid. Everything is a complete blank.
Duke (*covering his relief*) I see. And you can't remember anything at all?

Act I, Scene 3

Prince Not a thing.
Duke How fortunate — I mean, unfortunate.
Cinders I've sent for help, but in the meantime is there anything you can do?
Duke Me? Oh, no. I am awaiting the arrival of Prince Charming.
Prince Prince who?
Cinders Prince Charming. We're expecting his return at any moment.
Prince I see. Well ... (*He sways and holds his head*) Oh! I feel a bit dizzy!
Cinders I think you'd better sit down.

Cinders guides the Prince to one of the tree stumps and helps him to sit down

Duke (*to the audience; with an evil chuckle*) Hee! Hee! What a stroke of luck. The fool can't remember who he is. That saves me the trouble of having to lock him up.

Archie pops his head out near the Duke

Archie Can I come out now, Nunkie?
Duke (*snarling at him*) No!

The Duke pushes Archie out, then exits himself L

Cinders (*turning*) Perhaps you could ... Oh! He's gone. (*Going back to the Prince*) How are you feeling now?
Prince Better, thanks. This Prince you spoke of. What did you say his name was?
Cinders Charming.
Prince (*laughing*) It seems an odd sort of name.
Cinders No odder than mine.
Prince But Cinderella is a lovely name. And you suit it so well.
Cinders (*embarrassed*) Thank you.

The Prince stands up and is a bit wobbly. Cinders goes to his assistance, and he puts his arm around her. They gaze into each other's eyes

Mattie and Hattie noisily enter R

The Prince and Cinders part

The Baroness and Baron enter R *and the Townsfolk enter at the back and sides of the stage, carrying flags*

Baroness Cinderella! What is the meaning of this? (*To the Prince*) Who are you?
Prince (*shrugging*) I haven't the least idea.
Baroness What?
Cinders He's lost his memory.
Prince It's perfectly true. I can't remember who I am, or how I got here.
Baron You haven't been to the (*local pub*), have you? (*Noticing the Baroness glaring at him*) Sorry, dear.
Baroness (*to the Prince*) Well, we can't have any of that sort of thing now. We're expecting Prince Charming at any moment. Go back to where you came from.
Prince But I can't remember where I came from!
Baroness Then just — (*gesturing*) go *away*!
Cinders You can't send him away in this state. Can't he stay with us? Just until his memory returns?
Baroness (*outraged*) Stay with us! A prefect stranger who doesn't even know his own name! Don't be absurd, girl!
Prince I would be quite willing to work for you. Without wages.
Baroness It's out of the question.
Baron We haven't got a Buttons any more, dear. You sacked the old one. You could give *him* the job.
Baroness Well ...
Cinders Oh, please!
Baroness You say you are willing to work for nothing?
Prince Yes. Just so I can have a roof over my head.
Baroness Very well. You may take the position.

The Prince and Cinders are delighted by this

The Duke enters DL

Duke Pay attention! Pay attention all of you! Prince Charming has now arrived and is waiting to be greeted by his loyal subjects!

There is general excitement. The Sisters preen themselves. The Baroness makes sure the Baron is presentable

(*Announcing*) May I present — His Royal Highness, Prince Charming of Pantomania!

A grand fanfare sounds

Archie enters, backwards, from DL. *The others are silent. He is not what they expected*

Act I, Scene 3   31

(*Observing their apprehension*) Three cheers for his Royal Highness! Hip! Hip!

The others cheer and wave their flags. This startles Archie. He looks around to see who is being cheered. When he realizes it is meant for him, he is puzzled, embarrassed and confused. When the cheering stops there is an ominous silence

Aren't you going to say something? (*Nudging Archie*) Your Highness!
Archie Oh! (*To the others; in a rehearsed and stilted manner*) Greetings to you all, my soil lubjects — er ... loyal subjects. It gives me enormous pressure — er ... pleasure to be with you once more. (*Aside; to Duke*) Was that all right, Nunkie?
Duke (*aside*) Quiet, you fool!

The Baroness approaches Archie and does a curtsy. Archie does one back

Baroness Your Highness! Welcome home. I am Baroness Beaujolais. Allow me to present my daughters, Mattie and Hattie.

The Sisters advance on Archie, who backs nervously away. They perform their awkward curtsies, and then stand there with big cheesy grins

Archie (*aside; to the Duke*) What shall I do to them?
Duke (*aside*) Be nice.
Archie (*grimacing*) Oh, I say! (*to the Sisters; giving them a pathetic wave*) Hello!

Mattie and Hattie are taken aback and get into a huddle

Mattie He's hardly Johnny Depp, is he?
Hattie More like Johnny Vegas!
Mattie Still, he's a prince and I'm gonna bag 'im!
Hattie Y'mean, *I* am!
Mattie *I* am!
Baroness (*stepping in*) Girls! Girls! (*To Archie*) They're so eager to please. This is my husband. (*Pulling the Baron over*) Baron Beaujolais.
Baron Welcome home, Your Highness. Are you going to have a knees-up?
Baroness Don't be vulgar, Cedric!
Baron I mean are you going to have a party? To celebrate your return home?

This arouses general interest

Archie A party? I hadn't thought of that. What a jolly good idea.

There is even more general interest. The Duke is obviously not pleased with this

Duke Is that wise, Your Highness? Think of the expense.
Archie Oh, hang the expense. (*Getting carried away*) I say! Why don't we make it a *grand ball*! And we'll hold it tonight at the royal palace! Everyone is invited!

There is great delight and excitement

Baroness A grand ball! Oh, girls! How thrilling!
Mattie (*excited*) Come on, Sis! Let's get home and make ourselves look even more beautiful!
Hattie In that case we'll need to stop at B&Q (*or local DIY store*) on the way.
Mattie Whatever for?
Hattie We've run out of paint and polyfilla!

They rush out R, *followed by the Baroness and Baron*

Fuming, the Duke takes Archie aside

Duke A grand ball with everyone invited! What are you doing, you fool?
Archie I thought you wanted me to act like a prince, Nunkie.
Duke I didn't tell you to squander money on this rabble!
Archie Shall I cancel it?
Duke It's too late now. But in future you will not do a thing without my say so! Is that understood?
Archie Yes, Nunkie.
Cinders (*coming down*) Excuse me, Your Highness.

Cinders curtsies, and Archie does the same

> We have prepared a special song and dance in your honour. Would it be all right to perform it now?
> **Archie** Oh, I say! A song and dance for me! Well, I ...

Archie looks to the Duke, who gives him a curt nod

Act I, Scene 4

(*To Cinders*) That would be absolutely marvellous!

Song 6

Cinders and the Townsfolk go into their song and dance. Cinders can involve the Prince. It ends with a tableau using flags. Archie is clapping enthusiastically, much to the annoyance of the Duke

The Lights fade to Black-out

Music covers the scene change

SCENE 4

The Lights come up on the street (same as Act I, Scene 2)

The Baroness enters DL

Baroness Come along! Come along!

The Baron trots on from DL. *He is followed by Cinders and the Prince*

Do keep up!
Baron (*gasping*) Yes, dear.
Baroness Cinderella. You will see to it that our new Buttons is supplied with a uniform. You will also instruct him in his daily duties. (*To the Prince*) You will start work immediately. We shall also require your attendance at the palace ball tonight.
Prince (*pleased*) Oh, thanks very much.
Baroness (*with a icy glare*) To wait on us!
Prince Oh.

The Baroness moves to exit DR

Baroness (*to the Baron*) Oh, do come along, Cedric! Why are you always dragging behind?
Baron I can't help it, dear. (*Indicating his posterior*) It just seems to follow me about.

The Baroness pushes the Baron out in front of her, and then exits

Prince Well, Cinderella. With me working in the house I suppose we shall get to see quite a lot of each other.

Cinders I doubt it. My stepmother and her daughters will keep us both busy. They're very demanding.
Prince As bad as that, eh?
Cinders I'm afraid so.
Prince Well, never mind. I expect we'll have some time to ourselves.
Cinders I hope so.

The Prince smiles, and exits DR

Cinders (*gazing after him; she sighs*) Oh, I *really* hope so.

Song 7

Cinders exits DR

The Duo enter DL

Nip
Tuck } (*together; to the audience; gloomily*) Hello.
Tuck We're not happy bunnies, are we, Nip?
Nip No. That rotten Duke made us lock poor Buttons in the palace dungeon.
Tuck And he's got Archie pretending to be Prince Charming.
Nip We dunno what's happened to the *real* prince. Do you know, kids?
Tuck Yes. Let's see who's been keeping awake. What's happened to him?

With ad-libs and participation they get the audience to tell them about the Prince's loss of memory, etc.

Tuck I see. Thanks, folks. (*To Nip*) So, the Prince has lost his memory.
Nip Yeah! They call it magnesia.
Tuck It's got very complicated, hasn't it?
Nip Yeah! Worse than (*TV show or topical gag*)!
Tuck Well, we don't want to have any more to do with the Duke's evil plans, do we?
Nip No. We wish to wash our feet of it entirely! What are we gonna do?
Tuck A runner! That's what we're gonna do!

They make for the exit DR, *but the Duke enters from* DL, *causing them to freeze in their tracks*

Act I, Scene 4

Duke Ah! You two! (*Approaching the Duo*) Is that fool safely locked up in the dungeon?

Nip
Tuck } (*together*) Yes, sir.

Archie enters DL. *He parades across the front, doing the royal wave*

Duke You can stop doing that now, you idiot. There's no one here.

Archie (*pointing to the audience*) Oh, yes, there is. (*He gives the audience a wave*)

Duke (*to the audience; sneering*) Bah! They don't matter.

Archie Nunkie, how long do I have to go on pretending to be the Prince?

Duke Until you are crowned King.

Archie (*gulping*) King! Oh, I say! I couldn't do that. That'd be frightfully dishonest.

Duke (*grabbing him*) Listen to me, you halfwit! You *will* be crowned King. And when you are, you will do exactly as I tell you. *I* shall still be ruling this country. You will just be my puppet.

Archie Poppet?

Duke Puppet! I shall be working you from behind!

Archie (*moving away*) Oh, I say!

Duke You will take your orders from me.

Archie But ... but that's very naughty, Nunkie. (*Showing a spark of defiance*) Suppose I tell people the truth?

Duke Then you will be arrested for impersonating a member of the royal family. That is high treason and punishable — *by death*!

Archie Oh, I say!

Duke So you will keep your mouth shut and do what I tell you. Understand?

Archie Yes, Nunkie.

Duke Now let us return to the palace. We have to make arrangements for this extravagant ball you have seen fit to inflict on us.

Archie (*brightening up*) Oh, yes! I'm really looking forward to the ball.

Duke (*smirking*) Well, make the most of it. (*Snarling*) There won't be another one!

Archie (*deflated*) Oh, pity.

Duke (*moving* DL) Come along!

Archie follows, giving the audience the royal wave. The Duke pushes Archie out DL

The Duo start to sneak out DR

(*Spotting them*) Where do you think you're going?

The Duo freeze in their tracks

Keep a close watch on him! Make sure he doesn't say anything he shouldn't.

The Duo give the audience a despairing look, then cross and exit DL

(*To the audience; with his evil chuckle*) Hee! Hee! My ingenious plan has worked. I have fooled these cretins completely. No one suspects that that buffoon isn't the real Prince Charming. He is such a colossal nincompoop I can manipulate him any way I choose. And the real Prince is no threat to me because he can't remember who he is! (*He gives his evil laugh*) Ha! Ha! Ha! Oh, you must admit it! I'm very, *very* clever! Oh, yes, I am!
Audience Oh, no, you're not!
Duke Oh, yes, I am!
Audience Oh, no, you're not!
Duke Oh, yes, I am
Audience Oh, no, you're not!

The Duke exits DL

The Lights fade to Black-out

Music covers the scene change

Scene 5

The Lights come up on the Sisters' dressing-room

Half-set. Backcloth and side wings show wardrobes and dressers overflowing with dresses, underwear and hats, etc. There are dressing tables and stools R *and* L. *These have prop mirrors and are loaded with make-up and cosmetic paraphernalia*

Mattie is seated R *and Hattie is seated* L. *Both wear voluminous dressing gowns*

A slapstick routine for the Sisters opens the scene. (See Production Notes) At some point they remove their dressing gowns to reveal ludicrous underwear. Comic business ensues as they put on corsets

Act I, Scene 5

After the routine, a knock is heard off R

Mattie (*calling*) Who is it?
Prince (*off* R) The new Buttons!
Hattie (*calling*) You can't come in!
Mattie (*calling*) We're not decent!
Prince (*off* R) Your invitations for the ball have just arrived.

The Sisters squeal with delight. Comic business as they both try to get into the same dressing gown. Eventually they sort themselves out

Mattie (*bellowing*) Ready!
Hattie (*squawking*) You can come in now!

The Prince enters R. *He now wears a natty (Principal Boy) version of Buttons' uniform with fishnet tights. He carries three large shiny invitation cards*

Ooh! Look! It's (*something comically appropriate to suit the Prince's costume*)!
Mattie The top half's all right, but where's yer trousers?
Prince This is all that would fit.
Hattie I suppose you'll say, "I'm Buttons, but there's no flies on me!"

The Sisters think this is highly hilarious

Mattie Are those our invitations?
Prince (*holding out two cards*) Yes.
Mattie Give 'em 'ere! (*She snatches her card*)
Hattie (*snatching her card*) Ooh! Aren't they shiny? You can see your face in 'em! (*She looks at her card and lets out a scream*) Ahhgh! (*She shows Mattie the card*) Who's that?
Mattie (*looking at her own reflection in the card*) Me!
Hattie Thank goodness! I thought it was me! (*She fans herself with her card*)
Mattie (*to the Prince*) Who's that other one for? Is it Mummy's?
Prince No. I've already given the Baron and Baroness theirs. This one is for Cinderella.
Mattie }
Hattie } (*together; outraged and shrieking*) Cinderella!
Prince What's wrong with that?
Mattie But she can't go to a grand ball!
Prince Why not?

Hattie Why not! It's only for top drawer aristoprats like us!
Mattie And she's just a common little scruff bag!
Prince (*sarcastically*) Really? I thought she was your stepsister.
Hattie Huh! Only a *small* step!
Mattie The *bottom* step, in fact!

The Sisters hoot with laughter

Prince (*holding up Cinderella's card*) Well, she's got an invitation. That entitles her to go to the ball.
Mattie Is that so? (*She snatches Cinderella's card*) Give it 'ere! I'll tear it up! (*She is about to tear up the card*)
Hattie (*snatching the card away from her*) Stop! Don't do that! It's for Cinderella! Don't be so mean!
Mattie (*gobsmacked*) Eh?
Hattie (*to the Prince*) Be so good as to call Cinderella.

Surprised at this sudden change, the Prince moves to R

Prince (*calling off*) Cinders! Will you come here a moment!
Mattie (*taking Hattie aside* L) 'Ere! Are you feeling all right? Have you gone soft in your old age?
Hattie You wait and see, sister dear.

Cinders enters R

Cinders You wanted me?
Hattie (*overly sweet*) Hello, Cinders, *my dear.* (*Holding up the invitation*) Do you know what this is?
Cinders It looks like an invitation of some sort.
Hattie It is, my dear. It's an invitation to the Prince's grand ball tonight. And it's ... *for you*!
Cinders (*over the moon*) Really? For me?
Hattie Yes, my dear. All for you. (*Waving the card*) Come and get it.

Cinders crosses. Hattie is about to hand her the card, then gives a fiendish cackle and tears it up. She throws the pieces in the poor girl's face. The Sisters do a high-five and hoot with laughter

Near to tears, Cinders runs out R

Prince (*glaring at the Sisters*) That was a thoroughly nasty and spiteful thing to do!

Act I, Scene 5

Hattie I know! And I loved every minute of it!
Mattie Nice one, Sis! Oh! The look on 'er face!

The Sisters hoot with laughter

Prince You two are beneath contempt!

Fuming with rage, the Prince exits R

Howling with renewed laughter, the Sisters move forward. The tabs close behind them

Mattie Oh, that was great, Hattie! I really enjoyed that.
Hattie Me too, Mattie. There's nothing like humiliatin' the servants. (*To the audience*) We're the best, aren't we?
Audience No!
Mattie
Hattie } (*together*) Oh, yes, we are!
Audience Oh, no, you're not!
Mattie
Hattie } (*together*) Oh, yes, we are!
Audience Oh, no, you're not!
Mattie
Hattie } (*together*) Oh, yes, we are!
Mattie We don't care what *you* think! Nah!
Hattie We *know* we're the best! So there!

Reprise of Song 2 (Optional)

Reprise of song only if more time is required for the scene change

Poking their tongues out at the audience, the Sisters exit

The Lights fade to Black-out

Music covers the scene change

Scene 6

The Lights come up on the Baron's kitchen

Full set. Kitchen backcloth and side wings show fireplace and kitchen paraphernalia. There is a large pumpkin in one corner. (See Production Notes)

Cinders is discovered seated on a stool by the fireplace R. *She is weeping*

A large Cat enters L. *It crosses to Cinders and rubs itself affectionately against her legs*

Cinders Oh! (*Stroking the cat*) Hello, Puss.
Cat Meow!
Cinders Where are your kittens?
Cat (*calling* L) Meow!

Two Kittens enter L. *They frolic playfully about*

(*Sternly*) Meow!

The Kittens cross and rub themselves against Cinders. She strokes them

Cinders Have you come to cheer me up?
Cat
Kittens } (*together; nodding*) Meow!

With their mother, the kittens perform a short dance

Song 8

Cinders applauds them, and the three cats take a bow

Cinders You know they won't let me go to the ball?
Cat (*nodding*) Meow! (*She spits*)
Cinders But that's not the real reason for my unhappiness. You see, I've fallen in love with someone. He's the young man who has lost his memory. The trouble is, I don't know if he feels the same way about me. Suppose he doesn't, and if I tell him how *I* feel, he might laugh at me, or be angry and never want to see me again.

Cinders weeps and the cats try to comfort her

Prince (*off* R; *calling*) Cinderella?
Cinders (*standing up*) That's him now! You'd better go.

The Cat herds the Kittens off L. *She turns and gives Cinders the thumbs-up, then exits*

Act I, Scene 6

Cinders dries her tears and puts on a brave face

The Prince enters R

Prince Ah! There you are.
Cinders Hello.
Prince I've come to see if you're all right. (*After a slight pause*) Are you?
Cinders Yes, thank you.
Prince I can't believe how cruel those two are. The way they treat you is deplorable.
Cinders (*moving* DS) I'm used to it by now. It doesn't matter.
Prince (*following her*) Well, I think it does. They had no right to stop you going to the ball. (*After a slight pause*) Are you very disappointed?
Cinders I'll get over it.
Prince You shouldn't have to. (*After a slight pause*) I wish I didn't have to go.
Cinders (*with a smile*) And miss seeing all the dancing and festivities?
Prince I'd rather be here with you.
Cinders Would you really?
Prince (*moving nearer to her*) I think you know I would. (*Awkwardly*) Cinderella ... There's something I want to tell you.

Song 9

Romantic duet with romantic spotlights. After the number, the lighting returns to normal

Baroness (*off* R; *booming*) Buttons! We're ready to leave for the ball! Come along at once!
Prince I ... I'll see you later.

He kisses her and runs out R

Cinders moves to the exit and watches him go

Silently, the Old Beggar Woman enters L *and stands watching Cinders*

Cinders (*to the audience; elated*) Oh, he does love me! He does! He — (*Suddenly alarmed*) But ... but what will happen when his memory returns? Will he still feel the same way about me? Will he still love me? Suppose he is already in love with someone else! Suppose he ... Oh!

Cinders turns and is startled at seeing the Old Beggar Woman

(*Concealing her anxiety; pleasantly*) Hello again. Have you come for some more food? It's quite safe. They've all gone to the palace ball.

Old Woman I know. They wouldn't let you go, would they? They tore up your invitation.

Cinders Yes. How do you know that?

Old Woman There are many things I know, my child.

Cinders Well, it doesn't matter now.

Old Woman Still, It would have been nice to have gone to the ball, wouldn't it?

Cinders Yes, yes, it would.

Old Woman Especially as the young man you love is going to be there.

Cinders Yes. How do you know about him?

Old Woman (*smiling*) As I said, there are many things I know.

Cinders (*sighing*) Well, I'm not going, and that's that. It's no use wishing for things you can't have.

Old Woman Ah, that's where you're wrong, Cinderella. Sometimes your wishes *can* come true. That's why I'm here.

Cinders Who are you?

There is a flash of light, followed by a Black-out. There is magical music and sounds. When the Lights come up, the ragged cloak has vanished, and the Old Beggar Woman is revealed as the Fairy Godmother, wearing a shining fairy dress and holding a wand. A spotlight follows her

Fairy Godmother No celebrity I from off "Big Brother"!
   Behold! I am your Fairy Godmother!

She waves her wand. There is magical lighting

   Several Fairies enter. They dance about to suitable music and then group themselves about the stage

Needless to say, Cinders is overawed by this spectacle

                I have watched you grow since the day
                  you were born.
                I have seen you treated with contempt and scorn.
                This is not fair, and will soon be put right.
                Some joy will be yours this very night.
                That is my reason for making this call.
                Cinderella! You *shall* go to the ball!

Cinders Is this real? Or is it a dream?
                Are these wonders what they seem?

Act I, Scene 6

Fairy Godmother Believe me, my child, you are fully awake.
Now we must hurry if the ball you're to make.
Cinders Go to the ball in these ragged old clothes!
Fairy Godmother My magic powers will soon change those.
A handsome coach will speed you there.
Ah! That pumpkin will fit the bill of fare!
Also, you will need a coachman and horses.
Have you any pets on which to use my forces?
Perhaps a lizard and some mice?
Cinders A cat and her kittens. Will they suffice?

The Fairy Godmother nods. Cinders goes to the side

(*Calling off*) Puss! Puss! Do as she bids!
Come at once, and bring the kids!

The Cat and Kittens enter

Fairy Godmother Of these two kittens, so timid and afraid,
A pair of white horses will soon be made.
This cat shall guide them through the lanes,
For as your coachman she will handle the reins.
And now, an ending to anticipation,
The time has come for the transformation!

Fairy Godmother waves her wand. There is a flash

Cinders exits

To suitable music, the Fairies perform their dance. As part of the routine, they lift the pumpkin and place it UC. They then lead the Cat and Kittens up to the pumpkin. The Kittens are positioned in front of it, side by side. They seat the Cat on the pumpkin

All the Fairies dance around the group. It ends in a tableau, and then the Fairies move to the sides

Fairy Godmother Behold! The coach in which to send her!

The Fairy Godmother waves her wand. There is a flash, followed by a complete Black-out

The Cat and Kittens exit

The pumpkin is removed. The kitchen backcloth is flown. When the Lights come up, a glittering pumpkin-shaped coach is revealed, complete with two white Horses and a liveried Coachman. (See Production Notes) Magical music continues to play softly until the end of the scene

Now for Cinderella! In all her splendour!

Cinders is led on by two small Fairies. She is now arrayed in a magnificent ballgown, sparkling jewellery and slippers

The Fairy Godmother leads her up to the coach. One of the Fairies hands her an invitation card. The other gives her a domino mask that matches the ballgown

> Miss Crystal shall be your name tonight,
> This mask will keep the truth from sight.
> And now, sweet Cinders, before you go,
> A word of warning I must bestow.
> Enjoy your evening at the ball.
> Until the midnight hour doth fall.
> For at the stroke of that late hour,
> My magic charms will lose their power.
> This coach and horses will cease to be.
> Your dress will be rags for all to see!
> Hark to this warning and heed it well.
> Be wary of the midnight bell.
> So, until the hour of twelve has struck,
> I wish you joy and all good luck.

The Fairies help Cinders into the coach

> Off you go without further delay!
> Take Cinderella to the ball — Away!

The Fairy Godmother waves her wand. The music swells as the coach starts to move off

CURTAIN

ACT II
Scene 1

The palace ballroom

Full set. Sumptuous setting. There is a rostrum across the back with balustrade and steps C. *In the* C *of the back wall is a large clock with movable hands. There are also palace side wings and a few small gilt chairs at the sides*

The Guests are on stage. They perform a stately gavotte, accompanied by singing

Song 10

A very dignified Major-Domo enters on the rostrum. He bangs his stick

The Guests move to the sides and turn US

Major-Domo (*announcing*) His Royal Highness, Prince Charming of Pantomania! (*He bows towards* R)

A fanfare sounds

Archie enters, backwards, on the rostrum from L. *He is elaborately dressed with a powered wig and orders. He backs into the Major-Domo and almost knocks him over*

Archie Whoops! Sorry, old thing!
Guests (*cheering and waving*) Hurray! Hurray!
Archie (*seeing the ensemble*) Oh, I say! Was that for me?

He comes down the steps, giving the royal wave to the Guests and the audience. He moves to DL

The Major-Domo bangs his stick

Major-Domo (*announcing*) His Grace, the Duke of Verruca!

There are groans and murmurs of discontent from the Guests

The Duke enters on the rostrum from R. *He wears his customary black with sash and orders. He is followed by the Duo. They wear distinctive coloured cloaks and hats with tall plumes*

The Duke comes down the steps. The Duo follow and stand to each side of the steps

The Major-Domo exits R

Duke (*enjoying the animosity of the Guests and the audience*) Ah! It's nice to see I'm still as popular as ever. (*To the audience*) What are you doing here? I don't recall any of you being invited to the ball. Gatecrashers! Get out, before I have you thrown out! (*By-play with the audience*)
Archie I say! They don't seem to like you very much, do they?
Duke (*to the audience; sneering*) The feeling is mutual!
Archie I think they're a jolly nice bunch. (*Pointing someone out*) Particularly *that* one. Awfully chummy sort.
Duke Bah!
Archie Try and be nice, there's a good Dukey.

The Duke scowls and moves away

First Guest (*coming forward with some others*) Your Highness?
Archie Who? Oh, me! Yes?
First Guest May we be permitted to ask what changes you propose to make?
Archie Well, I was thinking of having this room done over in pink with a nice ——
Second Guest No, Your Highness, we mean what changes you will be making to the running of the country?

The Duke moves quickly back down to Archie's side

Duke (*to the Guests; snarling*) There will be no changes to the running of the country! Everything will remain as it is! Isn't that right, Your Highness?
Archie (*to the Guests; weakly*) Yes.

The Guests are displeased by this and move away

Oh, dear! (*To the Duke*) They don't look very pleased, do they?

Act II, Scene 1   47

Duke (*sneering*) Who cares!
Archie Perhaps I ought to do something to cheer them up.
Duke Like what?
Archie (*brightly*) I could sing them a little song!

Song 11

During Archie's song he wins the Guests over and they join him

After the number, the Major-Domo enters on the rostrum. He bangs his stick

Major-Domo (*announcing*) The Baron and Baroness Beaujolais!

The Baroness enters on the rostrum from R. *She is followed by the Prince, holding the train of her dress. Annoyed, she turns and beckons to off* R. *The Baron trots on. She grabs his arm, and they descend the steps*

The Prince follows and remains in the background. The Baroness goes to Archie

Baroness Your Highness!

She curtsies. Archie tries to do the same. The Major-Domo bangs his stick

Major-Domo (*announcing*) The two Misses!
Mattie (*off* R; *calling*) Yoohoo! Here we are!
Hattie (*off* R; *calling*) Fasten yer seat belts!
Mattie (*off* R; *calling*) Ready or not ...
Mattie }
Hattie } (*together; off; yelling*) Here we come!

Mattie and Hattie enter on the rostrum from R. *Their costumes are the most outrageous and comical yet*

They get stuck in the entrance. After much pushing and shoving, they both get on. They push the Major-Domo out of the way, and strike a pose in the C *of the rostrum. To "Hello Dolly" type music, they slowly come down the steps in mannequin fashion. This is spoilt when one of them trips up. The music changes abruptly to "Colonel Bogey" by Lieutenant F. J. Ricketts*

Mattie
Hattie } (*together; to the Pianist/Conductor*) And the same to you!

The Sisters parade around the stage, showing off their costumes. It ends with them C, *adopting sexy poses*

Mattie (*to the audience*) What do you think? (*Current well known model*), eat your heart out!
Hattie (*to the audience*) Have we got what it takes, or what?
Mattie (*adjusting a part of her costume*) I've certainly got something! I think it's metal fatigue!
Mattie Never mind that! Look! It's his royal icing!
Hattie Ooo! Let me at him!

They push each other out of the way to get to Archie. He backs into the proscenium arch. They do their disastrous curtsies, then Mattie pushes Hattie out of the way

Mattie I hope you'll have the first dance with me, your Royal Jelly.
Hattie (*pushing Mattie away*) I'm sure you'd rather have it with *me*, your Imperial Leather.
Archie I'm afraid I'm not awfully good at dancing.
Mattie Oh, I'll teach you! I'm an expert. I nearly got on (*TV dance programme*)!
Hattie Until they discovered she had two left feet! You put yourself in my hands.
Mattie I wouldn't! You don't know where they've been! Dance with me!
Hattie Dance with me!
Duke (*aside; to Archie*) Dance with one of them, or we'll be here all night!

Archie gulps and approaches Hattie

Archie May I have the honour?
Hattie Charmed ever so muchly! (*She makes a face at Mattie*) Nah! (*To the Pianist/Conductor*) Hit it!

Song 12

The suggested style is rock and roll. As the music starts, Hattie grabs Archie and twirls him around. After a while, Mattie wades in and pulls Archie away from Hattie and dances with him herself. Hattie pulls him away, then Mattie pulls him back. This routine is repeated and poor Archie is the object in a tug of war between the Sisters. The number ends with the Sisters posing over an exhausted Archie, who has collapsed to the ground. On all fours and gasping, he crawls to the side and collapses on to one of the chairs

> *The Major-Domo enters on the rostrum. He bangs his stick. All the others clear, and turn* US

Major-Domo (*announcing*) Miss Crystal!

> *Cinders, in all her finery and wearing the half-mask, enters on the rostrum from* R

Cinders comes down the steps and moves DC. *As she does so, the Sisters make catty remarks to each other*

Mattie Don't look now, but the Lone Ranger's just walked in!
Hattie Who's she? All dressed up like a dog's dinner!
Mattie I hate to see that! Talk about OTT!

Cinders moves to Archie, who is still sitting on the chair, getting his breath back

Cinders Your Highness. (*She does an expert curtsy, much to the annoyance of the Sisters*)
Mattie Show off!
Hattie Smarty pants!
Archie (*to Cinders; taking in her beauty*) Oh, I say! Miss Crystal! I'd love to dance with you but I'm a bit out of puff at the moment. Please feel free to choose another partner. Anyone you like.
Cinders Thank you, Your Highness.

Cinders moves around, looking at the ensemble. One or two of the males look hopeful. At last she points to the Prince

Prince (*incredulously*) Me?

There is consternation from the Guests

Baroness This is outrageous! You can't dance with *him*! He's just a servant!
Cinders But I want to.

Baroness Oh! Your Highness, I appeal to you!
Archie (*grimacing*) You certainly don't!
Baroness (*rounding on the Baron*) Aren't you going to say something?
Baron Yes, dear. What time does the bar open?
Cinders His Highness said I was free to choose any partner I liked.
Archie Yes, I jolly well did. (*To the Baroness*) So that's an end to it. Dance away, Miss Crystal, dance away!

Song 13

Music starts, and the Prince and Cinders dance together. This can be accompanied by the Guests singing if desired. The couple are still dancing as the Lights fade to Black-out

Music covers the scene change

Scene 2

The Lights come up on a dungeon cell

A frontcloth shows slimy stone walls hung with chains and manacles. There is a rough bench

Buttons is discovered, pacing the cell. He becomes aware of the audience and greets them

Buttons Hello, folks! Hi, kids! Long time no see. (*He looks around at his gloomy surroundings*) What a cheerful place this is, eh? It's worse than the (*local nightspot*) at chucking out time! That rotten Duke had me locked up here so I can't tell anyone what he did to the Prince. I wish I knew what was going on. The only person I've seen is the jailor, and he won't tell me anything.

The sound of jangling keys is heard off DL

Here he comes now! You wait 'til you see him! He makes Shrek look like Barbie!

There is the sound of a door being unlocked and opened

Urk, the jailer, enters DL. *He is huge, hairy and shambling*

Urk (*with a grunt*) Urr!

Act II, Scene 2

Buttons (*to the audience*) See what I mean!
Urk 'Ere's yer grub!

Kathy, a pretty young woman, enters DL. *She is carrying a water jug and a lump of mouldy bread*

Urr!

Urk lumbers out DL

There is the sound of door being shut and locked

Kathy Hello. My name's Kathy.
Buttons Mine's Buttons.
Kathy I've brought your food. It's only bread and water, I'm afraid.
Buttons (*taking the jug and bread*) Thanks. It looks, er ... delicious.
Kathy (*smiling*) Believe me, it's not.
Buttons No. I was just being polite. Tell me, Kathy, what's a nice girl like you doing in a place like this?
Kathy I have to work somewhere. It was either this or McDonalds.
Buttons (*holding up the lump of bread*) Not a lot of difference then. (*He puts the jug and bread on the bench*)
Kathy Why have you been imprisoned?
Buttons Because I saw something. I was with Prince Charming when he returned home. I saw him attacked and knocked out.
Kathy By whom?
Buttons The Duke of Verruca! He had me locked up to prevent me from telling anyone.
Kathy That's terrible. What's happened to the Prince?
Buttons I don't know. But I bet it's something pretty awful if that rotten Duke's got anything to do with it! I want to help the Prince, but what can I do? Locked up here like something out of *Bad Girls*!
Kathy I wish I could help you. But with Urk on guard it's impossible.
Buttons Urk?
Kathy That's the jailer's name.
Buttons Really? He looks more like a Tracy!

They both laugh

But seriously, I've got to get out of here and help the Prince. But how? (*He looks about him and sighs*) I haven't a ghost of a chance.
Kathy (*thoughtfully*) Ghost ... ghost ...
Buttons What is it?

Kathy It's just an idea. Urk is a terrible brute, but he has one weakness. He's very superstitious. He believes in ghosts and hauntings and that sort of thing.
Buttons How will that help?
Kathy Well, if we could play on his superstitions we might be able to trick him. Oh, It's a silly idea, I know.
Buttons (*enthused*) No, Kathy. I think it's a brilliant idea. All we have to do is pretend that this cell is haunted. While he's having the collywobbles, we can get away.
Kathy We?
Buttons Well, you're helping me to escape. You'll have to go on the run with me.
Kathy I'd like that, Buttons.
Buttons So would I, Kathy.

They gaze adoringly into each other's eyes for a few seconds, and then Buttons comes down to earth

Now, how are we going to do it? How are we going to make him believe this cell is haunted?
Kathy We could make ghostly noises.
Buttons That's a good idea! (*Deflated*) But then he'd know it was us.
Kathy That's true.
Buttons (*struck by a brilliant idea*) I've got it! We'll get my friends out there to help. (*To the audience*) You'll help us, won't you, folks?
Audience Yes!
Buttons All you've got to do is make ghostly noises. You know what I mean. You've all seen *Scooby-Doo*. This sort of thing! (*He demonstrates by making ghostly groans and howls*) I bet you can do better than that, can't you? Let's have a practice then!

Buttons gets the audience to make ghostly noises

That's great! Really scary! That'd scare the pants off (*current nasty*)! Now, I don't want you to do it until I give you *this* signal. (*He does a thumbs-up*) Got that? Great!

The sound of jangling keys is heard off DL

Kathy He's coming back!
Buttons (*to the audience*) Don't forget to wait for the signal.

There is the sound of door being unlocked and opened

Act II, Scene 2

Urk enters DL

Urk (*to Kathy; jerking his head towards exit the* DL) Out!
Buttons Excuse me, Mr Urk.
Urk Urr?
Buttons Do you think I could be moved to a different cell?
Urk Urr?
Buttons I'm not happy in this one. There's something very ... *spooky* ... about it.
Urk (*reacting*) Spooky?
Buttons Yes. I keep hearing — *things*!
Urk (*getting nervy*) Wot fings?
Buttons (*playing it for all it's worth*) Strange ... *ghoulish* noises!
Urk Noises?
Buttons Yes. Ghastly, weird, *ghostly* noises!
Urk (*looking nervously about him*) I ... I can't 'ear n ... n ... nufink!

Buttons steps back and gives the signal to the audience. They make the ghostly noises. Urk is terrified and soon becomes a gibbering wreck

Still signalling to the audience, Buttons and Kathy creep towards the exit DL. *Suddenly, Urk becomes aware of the audience, and his fright is replaced by anger*

Urk (*to the audience; growling*) It's you!

He sees the departing Buttons, rushes across and grabs him

Kathy slips out DL

Oh, no, you don't! Come 'ere! (*He hauls Buttons* DS) Fought you'd try to trick me, did ya? Fought you'd get that lot to 'elp you escape, did ya? Wull! You can't make a monkey out of me, see!
Buttons There's no need. Nature's done a good job!
Urk Urr?
Buttons You were pretty scared though.
Urk Nah! I was jus' pretendin'. I knowed it was them all along.
Buttons Oh, no, you didn't! (*To the audience*) Did he?
Audience No!
Urk (*to the audience*) Oh, yes, I did!
Audience Oh, no, you didn't!
Urk (*to the audience*) Oh, yes, I did!
Audience Oh, no, you didn't!

Urk (*to the audience*) Oh, yes, I did!
Audience Oh, no, you didn't!
Urk You can't fool me! There ain't no ghosts 'ere!

A ghostly shape in a white sheet (Kathy) drifts on DL

It moves to behind Urk, and taps him on the shoulder. He turns to look, and does a double take

Urk (*terrified; yelling*) Mummy!

Yelling with fright, Urk runs out DL

Kathy removes the white sheet. She and Buttons laugh

Buttons Well done, Kathy. (*To the audience*) And thanks for your help, folks. (*To Kathy*) Come on! Let's get out of here!

They dash out DL

The Lights fade to Black-out

Music covers the scene change

Scene 3

The Lights come up on the ballroom

Reprise of Song 13

The Prince and Cinders are still dancing together. The others are in the same positions as at the end of Act II, Scene 1. Finally, the dance comes to an end. The Prince and Cinders bow and curtsy to each other

Archie stands up and applauds them. The Prince returns to the background, and Cinders mingles with the Guests. The Baroness and the Sisters form a fawning group around Archie. This makes him feel uncomfortable

Archie (*for want of something to say*) I say! That Miss Crystal is an awfully good dancer, isn't she?
Mattie D'you think so? She's a bit stiff, if you ask me. When *I* dance I like *all* my bits to move.

Act II, Scene 3   55

Hattie *Everything* moves when *you* dance, dear. It's like being caught in the middle of an earthquake.

The Duke crosses and brings Archie DS, *well out of earshot*

Duke Listen. Judging by her exquisite dress and fabulous jewels, Miss Crystal must be a very wealthy young woman. She is probably a foreign princess travelling incognito.
Archie In a Cognito? Is that better than the new (*car reference*)?
Duke Fool! It means she is concealing her true identity. Listen carefully. I want you to be very charming to her tonight. In fact, I want you to woo her.
Archie Woo? Who?
Duke You!
Archie Ooo!
Duke Your marriage to her would be most advantageous.
Archie (*with a loud squawk*) Marriage!
Duke Shh! Once you are married all her riches will be mine! *Mine!* (*He gives an evil chuckle*) Hee! Hee!
Archie That's all very well, Nunkie, but what do I get out of being married to her?
Duke Well, you'll be able to ... (*Giving Archie a look*) No, perhaps not!

The Major-Domo enters on the rostrum. He bangs his stick

Everyone turns US

Major-Domo (*announcing*) Supper is now being served in the banqueting hall!

Major-Domo exits

The Guests move towards the exit R

Mattie (*yelling*) Grub's up!
Hattie (*yelling*) Gangway!

Pushing the Guests out of the way, the Sisters rush out R. *The Guests exit* R, *men escorting women*

Baroness (*to the Baron*) Give me your arm.
Baron (*nervously*) Why, dear? What are you going to do with it?

Baroness Take me in to supper!

The Baroness grabs the Baron's arm and hauls him out R

Duke (*aside; to Archie*) Now's your chance to get acquainted with her. (*Nodding towards Cinders*) Take her in to supper. (*Nudging Archie*) Go on!
Archie (*approaching Cinders, awkwardly*) H — hello, again.
Cinders Your Highness.

She curtsies. Archie does the same

Archie May I suck you in to tupper? I mean, take you in to supper?
Cinders Thank you, Your Highness.

After a few comical contortions, Archie succeeds in taking Cinders' arm. He leads her out R. *With a sneer at the audience, the Duke follows them out*

Tuck Now's our chance! Run for it!

The Duo start to run up the steps

The Duke enters from R

Duke (*snarling*) Where are you two going?

The Duo freeze

In here!

Cowering, the Duo follow the Duke out R

The Prince moves to the exit R, *and looks off*

Prince It was very nice of Miss Crystal to choose me to dance with. I wonder why she did that when she had the pick of all the others? It's very odd, but while we were dancing together I had the strangest feeling we'd met somewhere before.

Pondering this, he continues to look off R

Buttons and Kathy poke their heads out from behind the wings on L

Act II, Scene 3

Buttons (*to the audience; whispering*) Hello, folks! Hi, kids! Is the coast clear?
Audience Yes!

Buttons and Kathy creep on

Look! There's the Prince!

They move over to the Prince

Your Highness.
Prince (*turning and seeing them*) Oh! Hello. Who are you?
Buttons (*puzzled*) Don't you recognize me, Your Highness?
Prince I'm afraid not. And why do you call me Your Highness?
Buttons Because you are Your Highness, Your Highness. You're Prince Charming.
Prince (*amused*) I'm sorry. You've made a mistake. Prince Charming has just gone in to supper. I'm Buttons.
Buttons I'm Buttons!
Prince Really? What a coincidence.
Buttons No, *I'm* Buttons! *You're* the Prince!
Baroness (*off* R; *calling*) Buttons! Come here at once!
Prince That's for me. Duty calls.

The Prince runs out R

Buttons What on earth is going on?
Kathy What's wrong? Why didn't he recognize you?
Buttons I wish I knew.

The Duo creep on backwards from R

Buttons (*seeing them*) Look out! It's the Duke's men!

Buttons and Kathy make a dash for exit the L

Tuck Stop! There's no need to run away.
Nip We're on your side now.
Tuck How did you get out of jail?
Buttons Never mind that. What's made you change sides?
Tuck We don't want to be part of the Duke's evil plan. After what happened to Prince Charming we're gonna do a runner.
Buttons What *has* happened to the Prince? When I spoke to him just now he didn't even recognize me.

Nip He wouldn't. When the Duke knocked him on the nut he lost his memory.
Kathy Oh, dear!
Tuck And that's not all. He's got his nephew Archie impersonating the Prince so he can go on running the country.
Buttons This is terrible. We've got to do something.
Nip
Tuck } (*together; reacting*) We?
Buttons We're going to need your help.
Tuck Sorry. Count us out. We don't want to get on the wrong side of the Duke. He'll have us for breakfast!
Nip Yeah! And use our bums as toast racks!
Tuck We're off!

The Duo rush to the steps

Buttons (*going up to the Duo*) Wait! Give us your hats and cloaks.
Tuck Why?
Buttons If we disguise ourselves as you we might be able to sort things out.
Nip Suits me. I think they made us look really stupid anyway!

The Duo quickly take off their hats and cloaks and give them to Buttons and Kathy, who put them on

And I was right!
Tuck Good luck! When you've sorted everything out, we can be contacted care of (*local reference*)!

The Duo exit on the rostrum L

Kathy What do we do now?
Buttons For a start we must try to get the Prince away from here.
Duke (*off* R; *calling*) Nip and Tuck! Where are you?
Buttons It's the Duke!

They pull down the hats and pull up the collars of the cloaks. Facing front, they stand to attention and assume the appearance of the Duo

The Duke enters R

Duke Ah! There you are! What are you doing skulking about out here?

Act II, Scene 3

Buttons and Kathy mumble incoherently

What?

They mumble again

Those elocution lessons with (*local ref*) didn't work, did they?

They mumble again

Never mind that now. Are you sure that servant is safely locked up in the dungeon?

Buttons and Kathy mumble and nod

You'd better go and check. I can't risk having him escape and blabbing to everyone. See to it at once!

Buttons and Kathy don't move. The Duke snarls at them

Well, don't just stand there! Do it!

Buttons and Kathy turn and march out L

(*To the audience*) Those two dunderheads get worse every day! (*He gives his evil chuckle*) Hee! Hee! As soon as my numbskull nephew marries Miss Crystal all her wealth will be mine! Ha! Ha! Ha!

Laughing with evil relish, he exits R

Buttons and Kathy poke their heads out from L

Buttons (*to the audience*) Has he gone, folks?
Audience Yes!

Buttons and Kathy creep out

Let's try and find the Prince.

They creep towards the exit R. *Mattie and Hattie's loud voices are heard off* R. *Buttons and Kathy quickly move away to* L. *They repeat the business with hats and cloaks, and then stand to attention*

Mattie and Hattie enter R. *Mattie is munching a sandwich*

The Prince follows them on, carrying a tray piled high with food

Hattie If you eat anymore they'll have to widen the front door to let you out.
Mattie (*with her mouth full*) Mmmm! Mmmmm!
Hattie Didn't anyone tell you it's rude to speak with a full cakehole?
Mattie (*after a big swallow*) I said, I can eat as much as I like. I'm on a special diet. I lost *five pounds* last week.
Hattie Weight Watchers?
Mattie No, Ladbrokes!
Hattie Hey! Look! It's the Duke's men over there. Shall we try chattin' 'em up?
Mattie Why not. Any man is better than no man at all. Who said that?
Hattie (*Topical reference*)?
Mattie (*plonking the remains of the sandwich on the tray; to the Prince*) Here! Take that away! And bring us our puddin's!
Hattie Oh, you are common, Mattie! (*To the Prince*) She means our desserts.
Mattie Them as well!

The Prince exits with the tray R

The Sisters preen themselves. Mattie wipes her fingers on the back of Hattie's dress. They slink over to Buttons and Kathy. Mattie stands very close to Buttons, Hattie close to Kathy

Mattie (*to Buttons; in seductive voice*) Hello, big boy!
Hattie (*doing the same to Kathy*) All on your own, tiger?

Buttons and Kathy mumble incoherently

  There's no need to be shy.
Mattie I'm not going to eat you. I've still got to leave room for my dessert!

Mattie laughs and playfully pushes Buttons. There is no response from Buttons and Kathy

Hattie (*across the pair to Mattie*) Not very sociable, are they?
Mattie They just need a bit of encouragement.
Hattie You mean ...
Mattie Yes, dear! (*To the Pianist/Conductor*) Hit it!

Act II, Scene 3   61

Song 14

During this comic seductive number for Mattie and Hattie, Buttons and Kathy try to make their escape, but the Sisters keep dragging them back

Mattie Well! That was a complete waste of time!
Hattie It always works with the boys at the (*local reference*)!

The Prince enters R, *carrying two custard pies*

Prince Ladies. Here are your desserts.

The Sisters rush across and snatch a pie each

Mattie Oooo! Doesn't that look yummy! I can't wait to get my choppers around that! (*She looks at Hattie's pie*) Hey! Is yours bigger than mine?
Hattie Ooo! Don't be so personal!
Mattie The pie! The pie!

They compare pie sizes

Buttons (*to Kathy*) Now's our chance to get the Prince away!
Kathy How?
Buttons I've got an idea.

Buttons and Kathy move nearer to the Sisters

Mattie I'm sure you've got more pie than me. Swap!
Hattie Shan't!
Mattie Go on! I'll let you use my (*latest aid in cosmetic beauty*).
Hattie Oh, go on then!

They swap pies. Buttons goes over and peers very closely at Mattie's pie

Mattie Oi! Get yer nose out of my nosh!
Buttons I wouldn't eat that pie.
Mattie *You're* not goin' to! *I* am!
Buttons There's a fly in that pie!
Mattie A fly in my pie?
Buttons Aye! A fly in your pie!

Mattie There's no fly in my pie. You lie!
Buttons (*pointing to the pie*) What's that then? Crawling about! Ugh!
Mattie (*looking at the pie*) Where? I can't see anything.
Buttons Look closer.
Mattie (*looking closer*) No. I still can't see anything!
Buttons Even closer.
Mattie (*looking even closer*) No, still can't see anything!
Buttons Let me help you!

He pushes the pie up into Mattie's face. Hattie hoots with laughter

Hattie Look! It's Frosty, the Snowman!

Hattie continues to laugh. Mattie moves to her

Mattie (*with icy calm*) You think it's funny, do you?
Hattie Hilarious! (*She laughs*)
Mattie (*ultra polite*) Excuse me.

Mattie takes Hattie's pie. There is comic business as she pushes it into Hattie's face. Hattie lets out a squeal

  Not laughin' now, are ya?

Hattie scoops off some of the pie and throws it at Mattie, who throws some back. They chase each other US, *throwing pie at each other*

Buttons (*to Kathy*) Now's our chance!

Buttons and Kathy rush to the Prince and bundle him towards the exit L

  Quick! This way, Your Highness!
Prince But, what's ——

Buttons and Kathy exit with the Prince L

The Sisters move DS, *still throwing pie at each other and making lots of noise about it*

The Baroness, Cinders, Archie and the Duke enter R. *The Baron, now a bit tipsy, follows. The Guests enter and fill the back of the stage*

Mattie throws some pie at Hattie, who ducks, and it lands on the Baron

Baron Drat those seagulls!

Act II, Scene 3   63

Baroness   Girls! Girls! What is the meaning of this unseemly behaviour?
Hattie *She* started it, Mummy!
Mattie No, I never, Mummy! *She* did!

Mattie and Hattie start throwing pie at each other again

Baroness (*to the Baron*) Do something!

The Baron moves between the Sisters, and gets covered in more pie

   Stop it at once! What ever will His Highness think!

The Sister calm down. Thoughtfully, Mattie rubs the pie into her cheek

Mattie Mm! Y'know, this stuff is better than *Oil of Ugly*.
Hattie (*doing the same*) Yeah, you're right, Sis! (*She pops her finger in her mouth*) Mmn! Tastes better, an' all!
Baroness Go and get yourselves cleaned up at once.

The Sisters exit R, *still discussing the virtues of the pie as a face cream*

Duke Miss Crystal, His Highness has expressed his desire to dance with you. (*To Archie*) Have you not, Your Highness?
Archie Have I?

The Duke nudges him

   Oh, yes! (*To Cinders; awkwardly*) I'd like to get you on the floor — I mean ... do you fancy a little ... I mean —
Cinders (*rescuing him*) It would be an honour to dance with you, Your Highness.
Archie Thanks most awfully. (*To the Pianist/Conductor*) May we have a little tinkle, please!

Waltz music starts. Archie and Cinders dance together across the front. He is not very good at first, but Cinders soon gives him confidence. The Guests dance in the background

During the dance, the hands of the clock reach midnight and the sound of twelve striking is heard above the music

Archie (*as they dance*) I say! Midnight already! Doesn't time fly when you're enjoying yourself?

Cinders stops dancing

Cinders (*alarmed*) Did you say midnight? (*She turns and looks at the clock*) Oh, dear! Oh, *no*!

Pushing her way through the dancers, she runs up the steps and exits on the rostrum R

Everyone stops dancing and watches her hasty departure in amazement. The music dwindles out

Archie (*in dismay*) Oh, I say! I didn't think I was as bad as that!
Duke (*going to Archie and dragging him aside*) What did you do to upset her, you fool? I hope you haven't ruined your chances!

The Major-Domo enters on the rostrum R. *He is carrying one of Cinder's slippers. He comes straight down to Archie and the Duke*

Major-Domo (*bowing*) Your Highness. I feel I ought to inform you that Miss Crystal has just run away from the palace. In her extreme haste she inadvertently divested herself of this item of footwear. (*He holds up the slipper*)
Duke (*snatching it and waving the Major-Domo away; aside, to Archie*) Your future bride can't be allowed to vanish into thin air! She must be found at all cost! And this slipper will help us find her! Come on!

The Duke drags the confused Archie out L

There is an embarrassing silence

Baron It's gone very quiet all of a sudden. What's happened to the music? (*To the Pianist/Conductor*) Get your finger out, old chap/girl!

The music starts. The Guests resume their dancing

(*To the Baroness*) Fancy a quick one, dear?
Baroness I beg your pardon?
Baron A little dance?
Baroness (*brushing him aside*) Don't be absurd!

The Baroness sweeps out R

Act II, Scene 4 65

The Baron looks around for a partner, but all the ladies are taken. He sees the Major-Domo standing to one side. He gives a resigned shrug and goes over to invite him to dance. There is comic business as the Baron and Major-Domo dance together

The Lights fade to Black-out

Music covers the scene change

Scene 4

The Lights come up on the street

The Prince, Buttons and Kathy enter DL. *They have removed the cloaks and hats. The Prince is obviously grappling with the news they have just told him*

Prince So, let me get this straight. You're telling me that I am really Prince Charming?
Buttons Yes, Your Highness.
Prince And the Duke knocked me on the head causing me to lose my memory?
Buttons Yes, Your Highness.
Prince And now he's put someone else in my place?
Buttons Yes, Your Highness.
Prince (*laughing*) It's all too fantastic for words.
Kathy But, it's true, Your Highness. The Duke had Buttons put in jail to prevent him from telling anyone.
Buttons If you don't believe us, ask our friends out there.
Prince (*to the audience*) Is it true? *Am* I Prince Charming?
Audience Yes!
Prince Then it must be true if you say so. (*To Buttons*) Well, what do you suggest I do about it? As far as people here are concerned, I'm just a wanderer who's lost his memory.
Buttons We need to find somewhere to hide while we think out a plan.
Kathy (*looking off* DL) Look out! There's someone coming!
Buttons This way!

All three run out DR

The Duo creep on DL

Nip
Tuck } (*together; to the audience*) Hello!

Tuck We haven't got very far doing our runner! Thanks to him!
Nip I had to make sure the cooker was turned off, didn't I?
Tuck You didn't have to make yourself beans on toast first!
Nip Well, I was peckish!
Tuck Is there anything else you need to do before we go?
Nip (*grinning*) No, I've already done that.
Tuck Come on then!

They make for exit DR

The Duke enters DL. *He is followed by Archie, who now carries the slipper*

Duke Ah!
Nip
Tuck } (*together; freezing*) Ahhh!
Duke Well! Have you carried out my orders? Is he safely locked up?
Nip
Tuck } (*together*) Who?
Duke (*snarling*) Who? That servant, of course! I sent you to check on him!
Tuck Er ... Oh, yes! He's safely locked up! We'll go and check again, if you like.

The Duo make for exit DR

Duke Stay! I have need of you here. The mysterious Miss Crystal left the palace under very singular circumstances.
Archie Yes. It was jolly odd. I was dancing with her, you see. And awfully nice it was too. Well, anyway, all of a sudden she just —
Duke (*snarling at him*) Shut up!
Archie Yes, Nunkie.
Duke (*to the Duo*) As his future wife, she must be found.
Nip
Tuck } (*together; incredulously*) Wife?
Archie Oh, yes! Nunkie thinks we ought to get married. Me and Miss Crystal, that is. Not me and Nunkie! (*He laughs*)
Duke (*snarling at him*) Shut up!
Archie Yes, Nunkie.
Duke (*to the Duo*) It is obvious that Miss Crystal is a pseudonym.
Archie Oh, I say! There's no need to call her names, Nunkie. I think she's jolly nice, and ... (*Noticing the Duke glaring at him*) I know — shut up!

Act II, Scene 4   67

Duke (*to the Duo*) I am convinced that she is a wealthy princess who wishes to conceal her identity. She may now be using some other form of disguise. Fortunately, when she ran from the palace she left a slipper behind.
Archie (*holding up the slipper*) This one! Awfully sweet, isn't it?
Duke It will help us find her. Whoever this slipper fits will be our mysterious Miss Crystal. We must search every house tonight. She must not be allowed to leave Pantomania!
Tuck Search every house? There's hundreds!
Nip Especially with the new ones at (*local place*)!
Duke (*to Nip; snarling*) All the more reason to get started then! (*He pushes the Duo towards the exit* DR) Move!

The Duo exit

The Duke is about to follow. Archie is just standing there, admiring the slipper. The Duke grabs him and drags him out DR

Baroness (*Off* DL) Come along! Come along!

The Baroness enters DL. *She is jerked to a halt because the long train of her dress is still off stage. She gives it an angry tug, and the Baron flies on stage, holding the end of the train. He is still tipsy*

What do you think you're doing?
Baron Holding up your rear, dear. (*He hiccups*)
Baroness Put it down at once!
Baron Yes, dear.

The Baron finds his sleeve is caught on the train. There is comic business as he tries to extricate himself. He and the Baroness get into a hopeless tangle with the train. Finely, she pulls it free and the Baron falls over

Baroness What are you doing down there?
Baron (*getting up*) Getting up, dear.
Baroness This is deplorable! What has happened to that new Buttons? How dare he disappear like that, leaving me unattended?
Baron Well, I'm here, dear. (*He hiccups*)
Baroness And look at the state you're in! How many drinks did you have?
Baron Not many, dear. I spilt most of 'em! (*He laughs and hiccups*)
Baroness Well, come along! I do not wish to linger longer.
Baron No, dear. Mustn't longer ling — linger long ... ling ... lang — Oh, what you said!

They move to the exit DR. *She suddenly stops and he bumps into her*

Baroness Wait! Where are Mattie and Hattie? I thought they were following us. (*Alarmed*) Oh, I hope they're not lost! My poor girls! The thought of them alone is terrifying!
Baron (*aside*) How right you are!
Baroness What was that?
Baron I said they can't be far. Perhaps they stopped off at the (*local nightclub*).
Baroness Well, I hope you're right. Come along!

She turns to go, and Baron picks up the end of her train. She exits, pulling him off with her

Cinders enters DL. *She is now back in her ragged old dress and looking forlorn*

Cinders (*to the audience*) Hello. Well, as you can see, the Fairy Godmother's warning has come true. At the stroke of midnight all the magic disappeared and I'm back to my old self again. Poor, ragged Cinderella. (*She sighs*) Still, it was nice while it lasted. And I did get the chance to dance with a real Prince. But best of all, I danced with the man I love. Even though he didn't know it was me he was dancing with.

Reprise of Song 7

After the reprise, Buttons creeps on DL, *followed by the Prince and Kathy*

Cinders (*turning and seeing them*) Buttons!
Buttons ⎫ Yes?
Prince ⎭
Buttons Hello, Cinders.
Cinders What are you doing back here?
Buttons Looking for somewhere to hide!
Cinders Somewhere to hide? Why?
Buttons It's far too complicated to explain. Cinders, can you hide us somewhere?
Cinders Well ... In the house, I suppose. But, why are you —

Voices are heard off DL

Buttons There's someone coming!

Act II, Scene 4

Cinders Come with me!

Led by Cinders, they rush out DR

Mattie and Hattie enter DL. *They move to* C, *bickering as usual*

Mattie Well! A fine evening that turned out to be! Thanks to *you*!
Hattie I can't help it if men don't find you attractive!
Mattie They'd find me attractive if you weren't there to scare 'em off!
Hattie *Me* scare 'em off! It's *you*! You'd scare off King Kong, you would!

Urk lumbers on backwards from DL. *He stands, looking off* L

Hattie (*seeing Urk*) Talkin' of big hairy things, look what's just walked in!
Mattie (*getting excited*) Ooo! It's a man!
Hattie Are you sure about that?
Mattie Well, he's man enough for me!
Hattie He looks a bit rough and ready.
Mattie That's right! He's rough and I'm ready!
Hattie I saw him first!

Pushing each other out of the way, they move to Urk. Mattie taps him on the shoulder. He turns, and the Sisters adopt sexy poses. Urk reacts in horror and makes for the exit DL

Mattie (*grabbing him and pulling him back*) Come *back 'ere*! (*In a seductive voice*) There's no need to be shy! Now, what's a handsome boy like you doing out on his own?
Urk (*grunting*) Urrrrl.
Hattie He's just your type, dear! Straight out of *Mastermind*!
Mattie (*to Urk; seductively*) You seem lost. Can I point you in the right direction? (*She pushes out her chest*)
Urk I gotta find the Dook!
Mattie (*to Hattie; mimicking Urk*) 'E's gotta find the Dook!
Hattie He means the Duke. (*To Urk*) What do you want him for?
Urk I got bad noos!
Mattie (*to Hattie; mimicking Urk*) 'E's got bad nooos!
Hattie He's got a bad everything, if you ask me!
Mattie (*to Urk; seductively*) Well, I've got some good nooos. I'm completely free for the evening. (*Laying her head on his shoulder and fluttering her eyelashes*) I'm all yours!

Horrified, Urk pulls away, and runs out DL

(*Wailing and stamping her foot in frustration*) Oooow!
Hattie There you are! You've scared *him* off now!
Mattie Oh, shut up! (*Petulantly*) You're always pickin' on me! It's not fair! (*To the audience*) And you lot can shut up, an' all!
Hattie (*to the audience*) Yes! Sitting there like ... like ... like a lot of people just sitting there!

The Sisters have by-play with the audience, and then exit DR

The Lights fade to Black-out

Music covers the scene change

Scene 5

The Lights come up on the hall of the Baron's house

Full Set. The backcloth and side wings show panelled walls with quirky family portraits. Against the L *wing is a large walk-in cupboard. Against the* R *wing is a large open fireplace. (See Production Notes) There is an ornate stool to the side. There are entrances above and below the cupboard and fireplace. The stage is empty*

Cinders creeps on UR. *She looks about, and then beckons*

Buttons, Prince and Kathy enter UR

Cinders But, I don't understand. Why do you need to hide?
Buttons As I said, it's complicated. Just find us somewhere and I'll explain everything.
Baron (*off* DR; *calling*) Cinders! Cinders, are you there?
Cinders It's Father!
Buttons (*desperately*) Quick! Hide us! Hide us!

Cinders looks about. She rushes to the cupboard and opens the door

Cinders In here!

Buttons, the Prince and Kathy dive into the cupboard. Cinders shuts the door, as the Baron enters DR. *He now wears a nightgown and tasselled nightcap. He looks very shaky and his holding his head*

Act II, Scene 5

Baron (*groaning*) Ooo! I'll never touch that (*brand name*) again! Ooo!
Cinders (*going to him*) Father! Are you all right?
Baron Ah! Cinders, my dear. Your old daddy's not feeling very well.
Cinders Oh, dear. Can I get you something?
Baron A new head would be nice. This one's splitting!
Cinders I've got some headache tablets in the kitchen. (*Gently*) Come with me.
Baron Thank you. And Cinders — there's no need to shout.

Cinders leads him out UL

Mattie and Hattie enter UR, *and come* DS

Mattie (*indicating the audience*) Look, Hattie! They've followed us in 'ere! What a flippin' cheek!
Hattie (*to the audience*) Go away! This is private property!

A loud bump comes from the cupboard

Mattie Hark! What was that?
Hattie What?

There is another bump

Mattie *That!*
Hattie I think it came from that cupboard!
Mattie Let's go and look.

They creep up to the cupboard

D'you think there's someone in there?
Hattie How should I know! I haven't got X-ray eyes, have I?
Mattie No, they're just blood-shot! (*Indicating the audience*) Let's ask them! They think they know everything!
Hattie (*to the audience, as they move* DS) Is there someone in that cupboard?
Audience No!
Mattie }
Hattie } (*together*) Oh, yes, there is!
Audience Oh, no, there isn't!
Mattie }
Hattie } (*together*) Oh, yes, there is!

Audience Oh, no, there isn't!
Mattie } (*together*) Oh, yes, there is!
Hattie
Audience Oh, no, there isn't!
Mattie Well, I don't believe a word that lot says!
Hattie No. There's someone in there all right. Hey! It might be a *man*!
Mattie Then what are we waitin' for?

They rush to the cupboard, pushing each other out of the way. Mattie is just about to open the door

The Baroness enters DR. *She now wears a nightgown, robe and frilly nightcap*

Baroness Girls! Where have you been and why aren't you in bed?
Mattie We heard a noise, Mummy.
Hattie Yes, Mummy. In that cupboard.
Baroness Nonsense! (*Pointing to off* DR) Go to bed at once!

The Sisters exit DR

Now, where on earth is that husband of mine? (*Calling*) Cedric!

There is a loud bump from the cupboard

So! He's hiding in there, is he?

She goes to the cupboard and is just about to open the door, when the Baron and Cinders enter UL

Baron You bellowed, dear?
Baroness Ah! There you are! What are you doing messing about down here?
Baron Cinders just gave me something for my head, dear.
Baroness A brain perhaps?
Baron Very droll, dear.
Baroness I want you back in bed at once!
Baron (*eagerly*) Yes, dear!
Baroness I do not want my sleep interrupted any further.
Baron (*crushed again*) No, dear.

Loud knocking is heard off UR

Baroness That's the front door! (*To Cinders*) Well, don't just stand there, girl! Go and see who it is!

Act II, Scene 5   73

> *Cinders exits* UR

Who can be knocking at this time of night?
Baron (*gloomily*) Certainly not me, dear.

> *A loud bump is heard from the cupboard*

Baroness There's that noise again!
Baron Sorry, dear. Must be the pickled onions.
Baroness It's coming from that cupboard!
Baron Odd! I've never had it that bad before!

> *The Baroness goes to the cupboard and is just about to open the door*
>
> *The Duke enters* UR. *He is followed by Archie and the Duo. Cinders brings up the rear*

Baroness (*in a fluster*) Oh! Your Highness! Your Grace! We didn't expect you at this hour! Please do forgive my appearance. (*She indicates her nightcap*)
Duke I'm trying to! We need to search this house immediately.
Baroness Search the house? But, why?
Duke I'm looking for a young woman!
Baron Aren't we all!
Duke Miss Crystal.
Baroness You mean the one who left the ball so abruptly?
Duke The same.
Baroness Well, I can assure you, Your Grace, she is not in this house.
Duke I'll be the judge of that! (*To the Duo*) You two! Search down here! We'll look upstairs! Come on!

> *Duke exits* DR

Archie (*to the Baron*) Evening! (*To the Baroness*) Love the cap, by the way!

> *Archie exits* DR. *The Baroness sweeps out after them, followed by the Baron and Cinders*

Tuck Now's our chance! Let's hope nothing stops us from doing a runner this time! Come on!

> *They make for exit* DL

Mattie and Hattie enter DR. *They are now wearing ludicrous night wear and slippers*

Mattie } (*together; seeing the Duo*) Ahh!
Hattie
Duo (*freezing*) Ahhh!
Hattie Look, Mattie! It's those hunky henchmen!
Mattie Come 'ere, you lovely layabouts!

Mattie and Hattie advance on the Duo

Yelling, the Duo run out DL, *hotly perused by Mattie and Hattie*

The cupboard door slowly opens. Buttons pokes his head out and looks around. He creeps out, followed by the Prince and Kathy

Buttons This isn't a good place to hide. It's worse than (*local place*) during the rush hour!

The Duo and the Sisters can be heard crying and yelling off stage

Buttons and Kathy dive into the fireplace. The Prince is about to follow, when the Baroness enters DR

Baroness (*approaching the Prince*) Buttons! Where have you been? Why did you leave the ball without my permission?
Prince I —
Baroness Never mind! I shall expect a full explanation in the morning. Meanwhile, your services are required with the search upstairs.
Prince (*confused*) Search?
Baroness Come with me!

She exits DR, *followed by the Prince*

The Duo run on UL. *They dither, looking for somewhere to hide. They dive into the cupboard*

Mattie and Hattie run on UL. *They are confronted with an empty stage*

Mattie Where are they? Which way did they go?
Hattie (*to the audience*) Have you seen them? Do you know where they are?

Act II, Scene 5   75

Audience No!
Mattie I bet they're hiding in that cupboard! (*To the audience*) Is that where they are?
Audience No!
Mattie }
Hattie } (*together; coming forward*) Oh, yes, it is!

The Duo creep out of the cupboard, and sneak out UL

Audience Oh, no, it isn't!
Mattie }
Hattie } (*together*) Oh, yes, it is!
Audience Oh, no, it isn't!
Mattie }
Hattie } (*together*) Oh, yes, it is!
Audience Oh, no, it isn't!
Mattie I don't know why we're arguing with that lot. Let's go and look!

They go up to the cupboard and throw open the door

Mattie }
Hattie } (*together*) Empty!
Hattie I bet they're hiding in the fireplace. (*To the audience*) Is that where they are?
Audience No!
Mattie }
Hattie } (*together; coming forward*) Oh, yes, it is!

Buttons and Kathy creep from the fireplace and go into the cupboard

Audience Oh, no, it isn't!
Mattie }
Hattie } (*together*) Oh, yes, it is!
Audience Oh, no, it isn't!
Mattie }
Hattie } (*together*) Oh, yes, it is!
Audience Oh, no, it isn't!
Mattie Why are we arguing with them again? Let's go and look!

They go up to the fireplace and look inside

Mattie }
Hattie } (*together*) Empty!

Hattie I know what we'll do. We'll hide in there and pounce on 'em when they come back.
Mattie Very clever, Sis! You're not just an ugly face.
Hattie Thanks. (*She does a double take*) Eh?
Mattie Get in there!

Mattie pushes Hattie into the fireplace and exits after her

Cinders enters DR. *She makes sure the coast is clear, then goes to the cupboard and opens the door*

Cinders You can come out now.

Buttons and Kathy come out of the cupboard

Buttons Where's the Prince?
Cinders (*thinking he means Archie*) He's upstairs.
Buttons Let's fetch him and get out of here.

Loud knocking is heard from off UR

Cinders That's the front door. I'd better answer it.

Cinders exits UR. *Buttons and Kathy exit* DR

The Duo creep on UL, *and move* DS

Tuck They're not here, thank goodness.
Nip (*to the audience*) If you see those two ugly sisters, you'll give a shout, won't you, folks?
Audience Yes!

Mattie and Hattie emerge from the fireplace, and creep up behind the Duo

The audience shout warnings

Tuck (*to the audience*) What is it?
Nip (*to the audience*) Is it them? Where are they?
Audience Behind you!

A routine follows with the Duo turning round and the Sisters keeping behind them. This is repeated a couple of times. Finally, they come face to face

Act II, Scene 5   77

> *The Duo yell and run out* DR, *with the Sisters in hot pursuit*
>
> *Cinders and Urk enter* UR

Urk Dook 'ere?
Cinders Dook? Oh, do you mean the Duke?
Urk (*nodding*) Urr!
Cinders Yes, he is.
Urk Gotta see 'im! Hurgent!
Cinders He's upstairs. You wait here. I'll go and fetch him.

> *Cinders exits* DR
>
> *Urk moves to that exit and looks offstage*
>
>> *Yelling, the Duo run on* UL. *They are hotly pursued by the Sisters, in full cry. All four then run out* UR
>
> *Attracted by the noise, Urk goes* US *to investigate*
>
>> *Buttons and Kathy creep on backwards from* DR. *In this fashion, they move across the front. At the same time, Urk moves down, still looking towards the back. In the* C, *they bump into each other*

Buttons (*to Urk; bowing apologetically*) Oh, please excuse me.
Urk (*politely*) Not hat hall!

> *All three turn to the front. And then the penny drops*

Urk
Buttons } (*together*) You!
Kathy

> *Buttons and Kathy run out* DL. *Urk, whipping his club from his belt, chases out after them*
>
> *The Duo run on* UR. *They pause to get their breath back, and then disappear into the fireplace*
>
> *Mattie and Hattie run on* UR. *They cling to each other, gasping for breath*

Mattie Phew! In this state we won't be *capable* of doin' anything when we catch 'em!
Hattie You'll be all right once you get your second wind.

Mattie Second wind? I'm still tryin' to find me *first*!
Hattie I wonder where they are? D'you think that lot'll tell us this time?
Mattie They'd better, if they want to get out before last orders! (*To the audience*) Come on! Tell us where they are!
Hattie (*to the audience*) Are they in the fireplace?
Audience No!
Mattie (*to the audience*) Are they in that cupboard?
Audience Yes!

Rubbing their hands in glee, the Sisters go into the cupboard

Buttons and Kathy run on DL, *and straight out* UR

Urk lumbers on DL. *He looks about the empty stage. There is a loud bump from the cupboard. He hears it, and gives a deep chuckle. Brandishing his club, he creeps to the cupboard and throws open the door. Nothing! He gives a puzzled grunt, and goes into the cupboard. An ominous silence follows, and then Urk is heard yelling in terror. He bursts out of the cupboard, followed by Mattie and Hattie. They chase him out* DL

The Duo come out of the fireplace, and go into the cupboard

Buttons and Kathy run on UR *and go into the cupboard*

Urk runs on UL *and goes into the cupboard*

The Sisters run on UL *and go into the cupboard*

Cinders enters DR. *She looks about to make sure the coast is clear, and then goes to the cupboard*

Cinders You can come out now. (*She opens the cupboard door*)

All the others tumble out of the cupboard and fall to the floor in a tangled heap. After they have disentangled themselves and got their bearings, the chases are resumed. Urk chases Buttons and Kathy off DL. *The Sisters chase the Duo off* UR

Cinders is left alone and confused

The Duke enters DR, *followed by Archie*

Act II, Scene 5   79

Duke (*to Cinders*) Well? Where is this man who wants to see me so urgently?
Cinders He ... he was here a minute ago. I'll see if I can find him.

Cinders exits DR

Yelling, the Duo run on UR. *They are hotly pursued by the Sisters, in full cry*

The Duo and the Sisters run off UL

Duke What the devil is going on here?
Archie Is it sports day? (*Or local reference*)

Urk enters DL. *He is holding the struggling Buttons and Kathy by their collars*

Duke (*seeing Buttons*) What is *he* doing here?
Urk Thas wot I come to tell yer, Dook! 'Im an' 'er tricked me, an' 'e got out!
Duke You blundering blockhead!
Urk But I cort 'im! Both of 'em, see!
Duke Get them away from here before they ruin my plans!
Buttons And that's just what we're gonna do, you villain! It's time everyone knew what you're up to!
Duke (*sheering*) And how do you propose to do that?
Buttons Easy! (*Yelling at top of his voice*) Help! Help!
Duke (*to Urk*) Silence the fool!

Urk puts his hand over Buttons mouth. Kathy takes up the cry

Kathy (*yelling at top of her voice*) Help! Help!

The Duke grabs Kathy and tries to silence her

The Prince enters DR

Prince Hey! Leave that young woman alone!

The Prince rushes across and starts to pull the Duke away from Kathy. Urk pushes Buttons US, *takes out his club and hits the Prince on the head with it. The Prince falls to the floor, unconscious*

Buttons grabs Kathy, and they run out DL

Duke (*to Urk; roaring*) After them! Don't let them get away!

The Duke and Urk rush out DL

Archie Wait for me! (*To the audience*) I say! This is awfully good fun!

Archie trots out DL

The Townsfolk, in various states of night attire, enter UR. *They are obviously curious as to what all the noise is about. They fill the back of the stage*

The Baroness enters DR. *She is followed by the Baron and Cinders. Cinders sees the prone Prince, and rushes to kneel beside him*

Baroness What is all this commotion? (*Seeing the Townsfolk*) What are these people doing in my house? And what is Buttons doing on the floor? Is he drunk?
Baron If he's got any sense!

The Prince regains consciousness, and Cinders helps him to sit up

Cinders Are you all right?
Prince I ... I think so ... Oh! (*Holding his head*) My head hurts!
Baroness I'm not surprised! How dare you lie about on my floor in that drunken state! You are dismissed! (*To the Baron*) Show him the door!
Baron I expect he's already seen it, dear.
Prince (*to Cinders*) Who are you?
Cinders (*puzzled*) Don't you recognize me?
Prince No, I'm afraid I don't. (*He gets to his feet*)
Cinders (*to the audience; alarmed*) Oh dear! I think his memory has returned. (*To the Prince*) Do you know your name?

The Duke enters DL, *just in time to hear the following*

Prince (*laughing*) Of course I know my name! It's Charming. Prince Charming!

There is a reaction from the others. The Duke is about to turn tail, when the Prince sees him and calls out

Duke!

Act II, Scene 5   81

The Duke freezes

We met in the forest. You told me you'd been ruling the country in my absence.
Duke (*turning; warily*) Did I?
Prince You did! Be so good as to tell these people who I am. Tell them I am Prince Charming.
Duke (*determined to bluff it out*) *You,* Prince Charming? Preposterous!

The Duke reaches off DL, *and drags on Archie*

Here is Prince Charming!
Archie (*greeting the ensemble*) What ho!
Prince He's not the Prince! *I am*!
Archie Oh, I say! (*Aside; to the Duke*) I think the cat's out of the bag, Nunkie!
Duke (*aside; to Archie*) Shut up, you fool! (*To the Prince*) You realize this is a very serious offence! Impersonating a royal prince.
Prince But I *am* a royal prince!

The Duo run on DR, *obviously still being pursued. They pull up short at the sight of all the others*

Duke Ah! Here are my men! (*Pointing to the Prince*) Take this person to the palace dungeons and lock him up!
Prince You can't do that! I'm Prince Charming!
Tuck (*aside; to Nip*) He's remembered who he is!
Duke Seize him!
Nip But, he's ——
Duke (*snarling at them*) Do as I say!

The Duo move to the Prince and take hold of him

To the dungeons with him!

The Duo start to lead the Prince off

Urk *enters* DL, *holding Buttons and Kathy*

Urk (*to the Duke; very pleased with himself*) 'Ere, Dook! I cort 'em again!
Duke (*trying to push them off*) Not now, you blockhead!
Prince (*seeing Buttons*) Buttons? Is that you?

Buttons You recognize me?
Prince Of course I do! Thank goodness you're here! Perhaps *you'll* tell these people who I am!
Buttons With pleasure! (*To all; pointing to the Prince*) That's his Royal Highness, Prince Charming!

There is consternation from the others

(*Pointing at the Duke*) And *that's* a dirty rascal!

There is more consternation from the others

None of us knew what the real Prince Charming looked like. It was the Duke's plan to dispose of him before we got a chance. In the forest he knocked the Prince out, causing him to lose his memory. That fitted well with his plans. He then got his nephew, Archie, to impersonate the Prince. That meant he could continue ruling the country in his own nasty way!
Archie I say! That's jolly good! You're better than Miss Marple.
Duke (*snarling; to Archie*) Shut up, you fool!
Archie It's no use, Nunkie. You've been rumbled. You might as well own up.

With an angry snarl, the Duke makes for the nearest exit

Unfortunately for him, the Sisters enter there, preventing his escape

Prince (*to the Duo*) Seize him!

The Duo grab the Duke

Lock him up until I have thought of a suitable punishment.

The Duo drag the Duke out, amid boos and hisses. Urk follows them out

Baroness (*to the Prince; grovelling*) Your Highness! I hope you don't think I had anything to do with this awful business.
Mattie Highness? Since when was he a Highness?
Baroness We have been the victims of a terrible hoax, girls. Our new Buttons is really Prince Charming and the person we thought was Prince Charming is not Prince Charming but an impostor.
Mattie (*to Hattie; nonplussed*) I hope you're following this!
Hattie Clear as mud!

Act II, Scene 5   83

Baroness Your Highness, I trust that miscreant will also be punished for his part in this conspiracy.
Archie Oh, I say! I didn't want to do it. Nasty Nunkie made me! He wanted to go on ruling the county with me as his poppet!
Buttons I'm sure he's speaking the truth, Your Highness.
Prince Yes, I agree. He was just an innocent dupe. (*To Archie*) You are free.
Archie (*very pleased*) Oh, thanks awfully. That's jolly decent of you. There just remains the problem of what to do with *this*! (*He holds up the slipper*)
Prince (*taking the slipper*) A slipper? What's it for?
Archie According to naughty Nunkie, whoever that slipper fits will be my — I mean, your, future wife and queen!
Prince (*amused*) Well, it seems an odd way of choosing a wife. Still, there's no harm in putting it to the test. Buttons, perhaps you would care to officiate.
Buttons (*taking the slipper*) Certainly, Your Highness. (*He fetches the stool and places it* C) Right! Who'd like to try the slipper on?
Mattie }
Hattie } (*together*) Me! Me! (*They fight to get to the stool first*)

Cinders slips out, unseen

Mattie pushes Hattie away, sits and sticks her foot out. Buttons kneels in front of her. Comic business takes place as he tries to squeeze her foot into the slipper

Buttons (*to the audience*) Is there a tyre lever in the house?

Mattie pushes him away and tries to get the slipper on by herself. Finally, she holds up her foot with the slipper just perched on the end of her toes

Mattie It fits!

The slipper drops off, and is retrieved by Buttons

Hattie My turn!

Hattie pulls Mattie off the chair, sits and sticks her foot out. Buttons tries the slipper on her foot. To the amazement of everyone, it fits! She holds up her foot in triumph

It fits! The slipper fits! I am to be the Prince's bride! (*To the Prince*) Where's the 'oneymoon gonna be?

Mattie Not so fast, sister!

She grabs hold of the slipper and pulls. A false leg is revealed! (This has hitherto been concealed under Hattie's costume) Mattie pulls off the slipper and throws it to the floor. Hattie leaps up

Waving the leg like a weapon, Mattie chases Hattie off. The Baroness runs out after them

Buttons picks up the slipper

Baron I think you had a lucky escape there, Your Highness.
Prince There is another here whom I wish to try on the slipper. A girl dressed in rags.
Buttons You must mean Cinderella. Where is she?

They all look about

We'd better give her a call. (*To the audience*) Come on, folks!
Audience Cinderella! Cinderella! Cinderella!

Cinders enters

Cinders (*shyly*) Did you call?
Prince (*turning to her; playing a joke on Cinders*) Are you Cinderella?
Cinders Yes, Your Highness. (*To the audience; sadly*) He's forgotten me completely.
Prince I want you to try on this slipper.
Cinders But ...
Buttons Go on, Cinders.

He indicates for Cinders to sit. Buttons kneels and puts the slipper on her foot. Of course, it fits perfectly. There is a reaction from the others

(*Standing*) A perfect fit, Your Highness!
Prince I see. (*To Cinders; pretending to be disdainful*) Well, it seems I now have to marry you.
Cinders (*rising*) Just because the slipper fits?
Prince So it would appear.
Cinders And for no *other* reason?
Prince (*shrugging*) None that I know of.
Cinders (*moving away; crestfallen*) I ... I see.

Act II, Scene 6   85

There is a slight pause, then the Prince bursts out laughing, and goes to Cinders

Prince Oh, Cinderella! I was only teasing you. (*Taking Cinderella's hand*) Slipper or no slipper, I was going to ask you to marry me anyway! (*Drawing her to him*) I love you, Cinderella! I fell in love with you the moment I opened my eyes and saw you bending over me.
Cinders And I love you! I've loved you since ... since you were somebody else!
Prince (*puzzled*) Somebody else? I don't remember that.
Cinders Never mind! Just forget all about it.

They embrace. There is general jubilation as the Baron and Buttons congratulate the lovers

Song 15

Music plays. Led by Cinders and the Prince, they all go into a joyful song and dance. At the end the Lights fade to Black-out

Scene 6

The Lights come up

Tabs come down, or the frontcloth as Act II, Scene 4

Buttons enters

Buttons (*to the audience*) Well, that's it, folks! It's nearly over, kids. Ahh! (*He gets the audience to join in*)
Audience Ahh!
Buttons Everything has turned out great. Prince Charming is going to marry Cinders. And ... (*Going all soppy*) I'm going to marry Kathy! And that nasty old Duke is where he belongs. Behind bars!

The Duke enters. He looks very dejected and miserable. He doesn't even respond to the audience's boos and hisses

Hey! Aren't you supposed to be in jail?
Duke (*gloomily*) I wish I was! Prison would be preferable to the awful punishment the Prince has inflicted on me!

Buttons What punishment? You haven't got be a (*football team*) supporter, have you?
Duke Worse than that! He has ordered me to marry one of those ugly sisters! (*He groans*)

Buttons revels in the Duke's misery

Buttons Which one?
Duke That's part of the punishment! I have to go out with each of them for a month! After that time I have to decide which one I ask to marry me! Imagine it! A whole month with each of those horrors, and then to choose one for a wife at the end of it! (*Groaning in abject misery*) Oooh!
Buttons (*turning the screw*) And whichever one you choose, you'll still have the other one as a sister-in-law!
Duke (*groaning*) Oooh!
Buttons (*turning the screw even tighter*) And to make it perfect you'll have the Baroness as a mother-in-law!

This is the last straw! Wailing like a soul in torment, the Duke staggers out

Well, he certainly got what he deserves! That's what I call a really happy ending. No, wait! A *really* happy ending would be to hear you lot sing! (*He laughs*) You thought you'd got away with it, didn't you? (*Calling off*) Oi!

The Duo enter

Have you got the lyrics?
Nip No, we always stand like this!
Buttons The words of the song!

The Duo go off and return with the song sheet

The House Lights come up and a spotlight appears on the song sheet

Song 16

There is ad-libbing and participation as they have fun getting the audience to sing along. Children can be brought up and asked their names and ages, etc. The children are given sweets and return to their seats

Act II, Scene 7   87

The song sheet and spotlight is removed and the House Lights go down

Waving goodbye to the audience, Buttons and the Duo run off

The Lights fade to Black-out. A fanfare sounds

Scene 7

The Grand Finale

A special Finale setting or the ballroom scene can be used. Bright lighting and bouncy music plays as everyone enters for the walkdown. Mattie and Hattie are squabbling over the Duke. The last to enter is Cinderella and the Prince, magnificently attired

Prince	Cinderella and I are soon to be wed.
Cinders	I hope he doesn't bump his head.
Tuck	Old Nasty's plans have all been thwarted.
Nip	And now he's well and truly sorted!
Hattie	(*to the Duke*) If you marry *me* I will be your honey!
Mattie	(*to the Duke*) If you marry *me* you'll get more for your money!
Archie	Poor old Nunkie has got to choose.
Duke	Either way, I'm bound to lose!
Baroness	Which of my daughters will he marry?
Baron	If he takes 'em both I'll be happy as Larry!
Fairy Godmother	Our tale of Cinderella has been told.
Kathy	We hope you enjoyed it, both young and old.
Buttons	All is well, and she's got her fella, so it's a fond farewell from
All	(*waving*) Cinderella!

Song 17

Finale song or a reprise

Curtain

FURNITURE AND PROPERTY LIST

Further dressing may be added at the director's discretion.

ACT I
Scene 1

On stage: Front of **Baron**'s house
Housefront wings
Town backcloth and ground row

Off stage: Scooter (**Mattie**)
Scooter (**Hattie**)
Shopping bags full of clothes (**Cinders** and **Buttons**)

Scene 2

On stage: Street frontcloth

Scene 3

On stage: Forest wings and ground row
Forest backcloth
Tree stumps

Off stage: Clubs (The **Duo**)
Flags (**Townsfolk**)

Scene 4

On stage: Street frontcloth

Scene 5

On stage: **Sisters**' dressing-room backcloth and wings
Two stools
Two dressing tables. *On them*: mirror, make-up, cosmetics
Props necessary for **Sisters**' slapstick routine (at the director's discretion)
Protective floor covering
Two corsets for Mattie and Hattie

Furniture and Property List

Off stage:	Three large, shiny invitation cards (**Prince Charming**)
	Props necessary for **Sisters'** slapstick routine (at the director's discretion)

Scene 6

On stage:	Kitchen backcloth
	Kitchen wings showing fireplace
	Large pumpkin
	Stool
	Town backcloth or cyclorama for transformation scene
Off stage:	Prop coach and horses for transformation scene
	Invitation card (**Fairy One**)
	Domino mask (**Fairy Two**)
Personal:	**Fairy Godmother**: Magic wand

ACT II
Scene 1

On stage:	Palace ballroom backcloth
	Palace wings
	Large clock with movable hands
	Rostrum with balustrade and steps
	Gilt chairs
Off stage:	Stick (**Major-Domo**)
	Mask (**Cinderella**)

Scene 2

On stage:	Dungeon backcloth
	Rough bench
Off stage:	Water jug, lump of mouldy bread, white sheet (**Kathy**)
Personal:	Belt with keys and club (**Urk**)

Scene 3

On stage: Palace ballroom setting (as Act II Scene 1)
Hands of clock approaching midnight. (Needs to be synchronized with playing time of scene)

Off stage: Sandwich (**Mattie**)
Tray piled high with food (**Prince Charming**)
Two custard pies (**Prince Charming**)
Slipper (**Major-Domo**)

Scene 4

On stage: Street frontcloth

Off stage: Slipper (**Archie**)

Scene 5

On stage: Hall of Baron's house backcloth
Wing with large walk-in cupboard
Wing with large open fireplace
Stool

Off stage: Belt with club (**Urk**)
Slipper (**Archie**)

Personal: **Hattie**: False leg

Scene 6

On stage: Street frontcloth

Off stage: Song sheet (The **Duo**)

Scene 7

On stage: Special Finale setting or the ballroom backcloth

LIGHTING PLOT

Property fittings required: nil
Various interior and exterior settings

ACT I, SCENE 1

To open: General exterior lighting

Cue 1	At the end of Reprise Song 1 *Fade to Black-out*	(Page 16)

ACT I, SCENE 2

To open: General exterior lighting

Cue 2	**Nip** and **Tuck** exit *Fade to Black-out*	(Page 21)

ACT I, SCENE 3

To open: Forest exterior lighting

Cue 3	The **Prince** sings Song 5 *Follow Spot*	(Page 25)
Cue 4	End of Song 5 *Take out spot*	(Page 25)
Cue 5	**Archie** claps enthusiastically *Fade to Black-out*	(Page 33)

ACT I, SCENE 4

To open: General exterior lighting

Cue 6	**Cinders** sings Song 7 *Follow spot*	(Page 34)
Cue 7	End of Song 7 *Take out spot*	(Page 34)
Cue 8	The **Duke** exits *Fade to Black-out*	(Page 36)

ACT I, Scene 5

To open: General interior lighting

Cue 9	**Mattie** and **Hattie** exit *Fade to Black-out*	(Page 39)

ACT I, Scene 6

To open: General interior lighting

Cue 10	Throughout Song 9 *Follow spots on* **Cinders** *and the* **Prince**	(Page 41)
Cue 11	There is a flash of light *Black-out. Allow time for* **Fairy Godmother** *to remove cloak, then return to previous lighting. Follow spot on the* **Fairy Godmother**	(Page 42)
Cue 12	**Fairy Godmother** waves her wand *Magical lighting*	(Page 42)
Cue 13	**Fairy Godmother** waves her wand. There is a flash *Black-out. Allow time for transformation, then return to previous magical lighting with special lighting on the coach and* **Horses**	(Page 44)
Cue 14	The coach starts to move off *Fade to Black-out*	(Page 44)

ACT II, Scene 1

To open: Bright ballroom lighting

Cue 15	**Archie** and **Guests** sing Song 11 *Follow spot*	(Page 47)
Cue 16	End of Song 11 *Take out spot*	(Page 47)
Cue 17	The **Prince** and **Cinders** dance *Fade to Black-out*	(Page 50)

ACT II, Scene 2

To open: Gloomy dungeon lighting

Cue 18	**Buttons** and **Kathy** exit *Fade to Black-out*	(Page 54)

Lighting Plot

ACT II, SCENE 3

To open: Bright ballroom lighting

Cue 19	The **Baron** and **Major-Domo** dance together *Fade to Black-out*	(Page 65)

ACT II, SCENE 4

To open: Exterior evening lighting

Cue 20	**Cinders** sings reprise of SONG 7 *Follow spot*	(Page 68)
Cue 21	End of reprise of SONG 7 *Take out spot*	(Page 68)
Cue 22	**Mattie** and **Hattie** exit *Fade to Black-out*	(Page 70)

ACT II, SCENE 5

To open: General interior lighting

Cue 23	After the **Prince** and **Cinders** lead a song and dance *Fade to Black-out*	(Page 85)

ACT II, SCENE 6

To open: General lighting

Cue 24	The **Duo** bring on the song sheet *Bring up House Lights. Spot on song sheet*	(Page 86)
Cue 25	The song sheet is removed *Remove House Lights and spot on song sheet*	(Page 87)
Cue 26	**Buttons** and the **Duo** exit *Fade to Black-out*	(Page 87)

ACT II, SCENE 7

To open: Darkness

Cue 27	Bouncy music plays *Bright lighting*	(Page 87)

EFFECTS PLOT

ACT I

Cue 1	The **Duo** stand to attention *A fanfare sounds*	(Page 9)
Cue 2	**Duke**: "... Prince Charming of Pantomania!" *A grand fanfare sounds*	(Page 30)
Cue 3	**Cinders**: "Who are you?" *Flash of light*	(Page 42)
Cue 4	There is a flash of light followed by a Black-out *Magical music and sounds*	(Page 42)
Cue 5	**Fairy Godmother** waves her wand *Flash*	(Page 43)

ACT II

Cue 6	**Major-Domo**: "... Prince Charming of Pantomania!" *A fanfare sounds*	(Page 45)
Cue 7	**Mattie** and **Hattie** strike a pose C of the rostrum *"Hello Dolly" type music plays*	(Page 47)
Cue 8	One of the **Sisters** trips up *Music changes abruptly to "Colonel Bogey"*	(Page 47)
Cue 9	**Buttons**: "... and he won't tell me anything." *Jangling keys are heard off* DL	(Page 50)
Cue 10	**Buttons**: "He makes Shrek look like Barbie!" *Sound of a door being unlocked and opened*	(Page 50)
Cue 11	**Urk** lumbers out DL *Sound of a door being shut and locked*	(Page 51)
Cue 12	**Buttons**: "Got that? Great!" *Jangling keys are heard off* DL	(Page 52)
Cue 13	**Buttons**: "Don't forget to wait for the signal." *Sound of a door being unlocked and opened*	(Page 52)

Effects Plot

Cue 14	The hands of the clock reach midnight *Sound of twelve striking is heard above the music*	(Page 63)
Cue 15	**Baron**: (*crushed again*) "No, dear." *Loud knocking is heard* UR	(Page 72)
Cue 16	**Buttons**: "Let's fetch him and get out of here." *Loud knocking off* UR	(Page 76)
Cue 17	Lights fade to Black-out *A fanfare sounds*	(Page 87)

www.ingramcontent.com/pod-product-compliance
Lightning Source LLC
LaVergne TN
LVHW020354090426
835511LV00041B/3272